I0004817

Facebook
and
Other
Looming
Privacy Scandals

John Uwaya
Outstanding Security Performance
Award Finalist

© **John Uwaya** (2018)

First published in March, 2018

ISBN-13: 978-1987418613
ISBN-10: 1987418611

Credit for the cover background of this book is due: thrillist.com

Available from Amazon.com and other retail outlets.

About the Author

Mr. John Uwaya is the author of "Security Awareness: An Imperative and The Urgency" - the world's definitive book on the urgency of the moment - security awareness. The 400-page and 17-chapter literary work, made the finalists' list for the 2018 best trainer's Outstanding Security Performance award.

Postgraduate studies at the University of Lagos and professional training apart, Mr. Uwaya interacts with peers at global security organizations including the U.S. Department of Homeland Security (DHS), European Security Group, African Security Studies Group, International Counter Terrorism Officers Association, Israel Homeland Security, Physical Security Managers, Executive Protection Network and ASIS International among others.

Also, his practical experience has grown over the years by partnering global security firms that have included Texas Armoring Corporation of USA, D-Fence Electronic Fencing & Security Systems Ltd of Israel, Crewshield Ltd of England and Gaffco Ballistics LLC of USA.

Besides public lectures and peered reviewed publications, Mr. Uwaya's views on the subject matter of security are aired by the global print and electronic media. And this book is part of his public enlightenment efforts. He is presently based in Lagos, Nigeria.

Acknowledgments

More than ever before, no one can write an informative piece without perusing a gamut of literature made possible by an ever expanding body of writers. So, in the course of writing this book, I have had to consult numerous sources. While those sources have been individually acknowledged in the bibliography, the United States Computer Emergency Readiness Team (US-CERT) and Mr. Robert Siciliano deserve special mention.

Also, this work has been immensely enriched by extensive interactions with peers at global security organizations that include the U.S. Department of Homeland Security (DHS), European Security Group, African Security Studies Group, AEF Securite Globale, International Counter Terrorism Officers Association, Israel Homeland Security, Physical Security Managers, Executive Protection Network, Security Consultants in Nigeria and ASIS International.

Therefore, I thank all my friends at those professional bodies. As well, thanks are due Texas Armoring Corporation, USA, D-Fence Electronic Fencing & Security Systems Ltd, Israel, Crewshield Ltd, England and Gaffco Ballistics LLC of USA for a fruitful work relationship.

Finally, I thank my wife and children for their patience as I again, of necessity, scaled down my social interaction to get this book out.

While I can't but share the credit for this work with others, responsibility for any flaws is absolutely mine. And as every effort of this nature is a work in progress, constructive criticisms are welcome for improvements in subsequent editions.

John Uwaya (March, 2018)

Table of Contents

Preface

On 25 March, 2018, a privacy scandal forced Mr. Zuckerberg to apologize for a breach of trust involving sensitive private data of Facebook's patrons. Expectedly, global public reactions have been mixed and torrential. Besides negative investor and legal reactions, many Facebook users are reportedly closing their accounts hurriedly.

There could have been no need for such belated panic measure decision had such Facebook users known there is no anonymity on the Internet. And that apart from strangers being able to access any information posted online, how they would use such information is unimaginable. Hence before supplying sensitive information online, ascertain from the published privacy policies of an organization how your information would be used.

Many organizations respect customers' request that their information should not be shared with other companies or third parties. While Facebook's apology is admission of guilt that could translate to compensation for the offended, the damage is done and perhaps, irreversible.

That's why this book has been written to minimize if not eliminate chances of such irreversible harm. And for easy assimilation and understanding of the subject matter, the book is broken into the following chapters:

- ❖ Privacy Expectations: Asking for Too Much?
- ❖ Weaponry in Cyber Attacks
- ❖ Internet Connectivity and Security Issues
- ❖ Web Browsers and Secure Browsing
- ❖ Emails and Implications for Security
- ❖ General Computing Security
- ❖ Preventing and Reacting to Identity Theft
- ❖ Telephone Security

There is no prescribed order of coverage but taking the first three chapters serially would lay a solid foundation for understanding the entire book.

Chapter 1

PRIVACY EXPECTATIONS: ASKING FOR

TOO MUCH?

As recent as two decades ago, personal information in the public domain consisted only in addresses and telephone numbers. But these days, a considerable amount of personal information is on the Internet which has become a popular medium for communicating, researching and gathering intelligence on people. And regrettably, many people are throwing caution to the wind with online behaviours that render them vulnerable to criminal attacks.

No one can be anonymous on the Internet as strangers can access information posted online for use in unimaginable ways. **Pic credit**: pinterest.com

There is a pull of false sense of anonymity that is spurring people to disclose personal information which they would normally not share with strangers who could use such information in ways that are unimaginable.

That is the crux of the scandal about Cambridge Analytica using millions of Facebook users' personal information to influence their behaviour in public events including elections in a flagrant violation of Facebook's terms of service.

1.1 THE SCANDAL AND YOUR PRIVACY

The gravity of the privacy scandal is better understood from the tone of Mr. Mark Zuckerberg – CEO of Facebook's apology:

> "*We have a responsibility to protect your information. If we can't, we don't deserve it. You may have heard about a quiz app built by a university researcher that leaked Facbook data of millions of people in 2014. This was a breach of trust, and I'm sorry we didn't do more at the time. We're now taking steps to make sure this doesn't happen again*"

Also, the extent of harm to privacy is apparent from how the scandal is trying to sink Facebook in the quick sands of multiple lawsuits, governmental and official inquiries, and a massive #deletefacebook user boycott campaign devaluing the company's stock by $50 Billion within days.

The company has, also, been witnessing an exodus of business partners as well as advertisers including Mozilla – owners of the popular Firefox web browser, pulling ads from the platform on March 24 2018. SpaceX and Tesla CEO – Elon Musk have also joined the high profile converts to the #deletefacebook movement – deleting SpaceX and Tesla's Facebook pages over that weekend.

Reacting to the privacy scandal, Mr. Tim Cook of Apple Inc could not be admit:

> "*We've worried for a number of years that people in many countries were giving up data probably without knowing fully what they were doing that these detailed profiles that were being built of them, that one day something would occur and people would be incredibly offended by what had been done without them being aware of it*", he said. "*Unfortunately that prediction has come true more than once.*"

And users appear betrayed beyond consolation as evidenced by a massive #deletefacebook user boycott campaign which devalued the company's stock by $50 Billion within days. What a reflection of the painful injury inflicted on victims who might have forestalled hopping on the #deletefacebook wagon by realizing much earlier that no one can be anonymous on the Internet.

That much was honestly admitted by Mr. Zuckerberg in his apology:

> *"You may have heard about a quiz app built by a university researcher that leaked Facebook data of millions of people in 2014. ...We expect there are others. And when we find them, we will ban them and tell everyone affected."*

But you can spare yourself all that particularly on Facebook and generally, on the Internet. That singular objective is reason for this book.

1.2 THE SCANDAL AND YOUR SECURITY

Again, Mr. Tim Cook has this to say about security risks of privacy breaches:

> *"The ability of anyone to know what you've been browsing about for years, who your contacts are, who their contacts are, things you like and dislike and every intimate detail of your – from my own point of view it shouldn't exist."*

But that is sadly the situation right now where no one can actually be anonymous on the Internet. Apart from strangers being able to access any information posted online, how they would use such information is unimaginable. For instance, supplying details about your hobbies, job, family, friends or life story could arm criminals with sufficient information to mount an attack.

Publishing something online is like broadcasting to the world. Although you could subsequently edit or remove an information, members of the public may already have the maiden copy in their kitty or cached copies of removed web pages could still be available. That is why it is advisable to weigh both the pros and cons of publishing any particular information online.

Again, you are not anonymous during browsing sessions on the Internet. In fact, clues about your online activities are always retained. Apart from more general information like your IP Address, Domain Name, Browser/Operating System software and details of pages visited/length of time on each, more personal data about you can be captured.

But as the legitimate methods by which information are gathered about targets' browsing habits, use of cookies and spyware (full definitions ahead) is consensual. Also, while the easiest way for attackers to gain access to personal information is by asking and tricking you to comply, the choice is yours to be less vulnerable. Generally, avoid posting personal data in public fora because criminals are able to piece information together from a variety of sources to facilitate crime.

1.3 **PRIVACY AND SECURITY EXPECTATIONS: ASKING FOR TOO MUCH?** – Facebook, WhatsApp, Messenger, LinkedIn, etc are among the online social media that users enjoy their services gratis without a thought as to how their hosts or owners pay operational bills to remain in business.

So, because you are not paying for a service, the service provider may trade some of your information to offset costs of providing the service. And these days, clients queuing for intelligence gathered on you include governments – for tabs on national as well as global security. Hence the low points of free services bother on privacy and security of users' sensitive information.

By implication, the choice is yours to be less vulnerable because governments' reaction to breaches of trust could be expectedly cosmetic and might not be "well crafted" regulations as advocated by Mr. Tim Cook of Apple Inc.

1.3.1 Lax Privacy and Security as Bane of Free Internet Services - As the low points of free services bother on privacy and security of users' sensitive information, before supplying sensitive information like your name, email address, and other personal information on a website, take time to read a service provider's privacy policy or terms of use.

Ascertain if your name, email address, those of others in your address book or any of the information in your profile could find their way to other organizations. Needless to advise that you should outrightly "unsubscribe" from a service that is altogether silent about privacy policy.

Apart from InfoTech companies, reputable organizations gather and analyze data on individuals' browsing habits to ascertain the popularity of their websites or of some particular contents. Statistics gathered in the process are subsequently geared towards improving their website visitors' surfing experience.

Also, statistics on website traffic are used in marketing advertisements, sold out or shared with business associates or subsidiaries. That is why you should watch against being added to mailing lists by default. And if you cannot find any on a website, contact a company for clarification on privacy policy before submitting personal information.

Or find a site offering better security. Privacy policy verification should be periodic because they sometimes change.

But while many organizations actually respect customers' request that their information should not be shared with other companies, some websites exist either intentionally for crime or have been infiltrated by criminals for gathering more invasive information for malicious purposes.

Criminals do represent malicious websites as genuine and if you visit such sites inadvertently or fall for their planks on a compromised site, personal information like passwords, addresses, credit card information, etc. could be stolen for criminal purposes.

While, for instance, millions of people use online dating sites to enlarge their networks and meet potential mates, not all on those sites are sincere. Many are actually scammers hoping to win and lure you for either identity theft or physical harm.

Therefore, do not give your address, password, credit card information, etc. unless a site is trustworthy and with proof of information encryption. While ensuring that your security definitions for viruses and spyware are always up-to-date, never hesitate to abandon any suspect site promptly.

On the whole, at all times, a website's capability to protect against criminal attacks and restrict access to only bonafide recipients of sensitive information should never be in doubt.

An URL (Uniform Resource Locator) that begins with "https" as opposed to "http" and a lock icon at a corner of a web page indicate your information would be encrypted for protection. The encryption must take care of the transit and storage phases respectively for all-round protection (See pages 33, 36-7, 41, 56-7, 67, 71, 76, 78 and 80 for detailed coverage of encryption).

1.3.2 Apathy in Reviewing End-User Agreements (EUA) - On the sideline of the ongoing scandal, some Facebook users who downloaded their account data were shocked to discover that their phone calls and texts had been logged overtime allegedly without their consent. And Facebook's response according to one Mr. Paul Wagenseil, is that when those users consented to install some apps, they should have known that their phone calls and texts would be logged.

But although an EUA is actually a contract between users and a software developer, the later sometimes take advantage of users' tendency of hurriedly accepting default "checked" options without actually considering the contractual implications.

As legal contracts, EUAs may contain almost any conditions by developers and that is why original software as well as their updates or patches should be examined for any obnoxious terms. Apart from protecting the developer against liability or conferring right to install other software (updates or third party) on your computer, EUA may also contain other terms giving the vendor a degree of control over your device.

That could include permitting the developer to monitor your computing activities for transmission of information back to the vendor or to some third parties which could have serious security and privacy implications depending on what information is being gathered. So, seemingly lengthy agreements or those hard to understand could serve as caution to reconsider installing a software.

Yet, many users hastily click 'next', 'next', 'next' to blindly accept default options in utter disregard of prompts and EUA terms. In the process, they inadvertently consent to the installation of adware or intrusive spyware in their computing devices. Therefore, before accepting an end-user agreement, ensure you understand and are comfortable with the terms.

Otherwise, you may be agreeing to conditions that you would later consider unfair because of unforeseen exposure to security risks. Greater coverage of this particular topic would be found under Spyware Risks and Prevention on page 59.

Meanwhile for an effective mitigation plan, we must locate what has happened within the broader perspective of modern existence that depends heavily on computers, the internet and mobile cellular technology for communication, transportation, e-commerce, medical practice, etc.

1.4 **ENLARGED COMPUTER CONCEPT FRAUGHT WITH RISKS** - In fact apart from the traditional laptops and desktops, many electronic devices like cell phones and tablets are now full-fledged computers. Given the enlarged computer concept, the magnitude of personal information stored on your own devices and those of your contacts would be amazing.

All that could include information on residential locations, hobbies, interests, friends, finances, etc. which are all exposed to the same security threats facing all computers.

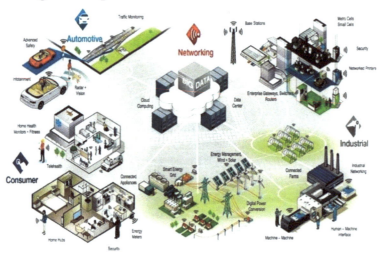

The Internet of Things: An enlarged computer concept fraught with risks.
Credit: channelregister.co.uk

Thus, the twin advantages of convenience and ease of connectivity offered by the ever widening frontiers of information and communication technologies do not come without some painful side-effects. And you are vulnerable even if your device(s) is merely part of a network - Ethernet or Internet. In either case, someone or something is exploiting your data for criminal purposes like the rude shocks of many patrons of Premera Blue Cross, Anthem, Home Depot, Sony, JPMorgan, EBay, Target, etc. in the recent past.

In desperation for access to credit card numbers, user passwords, confidential documents and emails, criminals successfully hacked into the networks of those corporations in the U.S. The non-classified emails of President Barak Obama and the State Department's network were neither spared in other darling attacks. And the mother of all cyber attacks till date is unarguably the one that has triggered a probe to determine any Russian influence in the emergence of Mr. Donald Trump as president of the USA.

In fact, use of the Internet, telephone, email and wireless connectivity is vulnerable to hostile surveillance with heavy users naturally more at risk. The sheer volume of data in transit and the potentials of successful attacks are reasons why criminals stop at nothing to acquire information for criminal ends. Neither is the wireless or virtual nature of connectivity that confers anonymity on attackers to remotely send or extract information without being noticed, helping matters.

Where corporate or public information are in a compromised personal device, losses could be collateral with legal consequences. In fact, criminals may sometimes not be particular about you but only want to seize and deploy your device as a launch pad to attack others who are most times high profile targets like governments, corporate bodies and international institutions.

That kind of identity theft could unfortunately expose you to the long arm of the law from which criminals themselves are hiding. Hence, it should be clear that even if connected to the Internet only for innocent activities like gaming or emailing with friends and family members, your device might expose you to criminal charges.

Criminals might want to expose you to the long arm of the law themselves are avoiding   **Pic credit**: guardianly.com

Therefore, good cyber security habits and adequate safeguards or precautions are imperative for drastic reduction of all known vulnerabilities. To that end, corporate and institutional networks are known to implement multi-layered security measures that include network firewalls and encryption. As well, support staff are on hand to maintain that security and guarantee round-the-clock availability of the networks. In terms of security, there lies the edge of an institutional network over one that is personal.

But as an individual, although your internet service is supplied by an internet service provider (ISP), chances are that no staff are on hand to oversee the security of your network or computing devices. So, you are ultimately responsible for securing your computers from accidental or intentional misuse.

To that end, upgrade the security features of your ICT devices periodically to guard or secure your communications. Similarly, modes of internet connectivity, emails, websites patronized, telephones and various electronic identities should be reviewed periodically. The next seven chapters proffer specific solutions for your safety online.

Chapter 2

WEAPONRY IN CYBER ATTACKS

The risks inherent in using modern communication technologies justify every effort towards secure communication at all times. Although the very best precautions may not guarantee 100% protection, taking certain steps can drastically minimize a target's vulnerability. And the first step in that direction is recognizing the risks by their basic terms or definitions. Broadly, these are hackers/attackers/intruders and malware/malicious code.

Attackers are those who seek to exploit weaknesses in software and computer systems for criminal ends. On the other hand, malicious code or malware is a collective noun for all software that are used by criminals to attack computing devices.

The risks inherent in using modern communication technologies justify every effort at communication security at all times. **Diagram credit:** Digital Security & Privacy for Human Rights Defenders

The following are names of the popular malware: "virus" destroys your software; "trojan horse" searches for personal identity/sensitive data; "spyware/adware" records target's keystrokes and tracks computing habits; and "worm" incorporates all three and exports target's vital information. Viruses often arrive via infected disks or emails; spyware infiltrate from both the Internet and Trojans; and worms creep in through networks or browsers.

While further details are provided as follows, it is pertinent to mention ransomware – the latest entrant into the fray of malware. As the name implies, it kidnaps a computing device for a ransom payment. Finally, some attacks are peculiar to corporate entities while others affect all and sundry.

2.1 ATTACKS PECULIAR TO CORPORATE TARGETS

The following forms of attack are particularly directed against corporate bodies:

a) **Backdoor**: Also referred to as a trapdoor, a backdoor is a hidden method of bye-passing security in order to gain access into a secure area. Backdoors are surreptitiously planted on a network element although sometimes installed on systems for a positive reason. An example is a craft interface installed on network elements to remotely facilitate system management, maintenance, and troubleshooting operations by technicians (called craft personnel).

Actions that craft personnel could remotely conduct include: initial switching on of network elements and/or systems, trouble verification, repair verification, monitor network element (NE) performance, update NE software and remote inventory. Although a craft interface permits a service provider remote access to troubleshoot and conduct maintenance on a system or network, a technician from outside a client organization could gain access to its system for cyber terrorist activities.

12

b) **Denial of Service Attacks (DOS)**: A DOS attack entails sending millions of requests every second to overwhelm and disrupt network traffic for a system to either slow down or crash. An even more lethal DOS is the distributed denial of service attack (DDOS) involving deployment of numerous computers to attack a target simultaneously. That happens when attacker(s) make zombies of unsuspecting computers by worm infestation before deploying them for a mass attack.

The overall objective of using multiple paths to overload a target with so many requests is to make backtracking an attack extremely difficult or impossible. For example, in February 2000 Yahoo, CNN, eBay and other e-commerce sites suffered DOS attacks causing over a billion dollar losses. Also, DOS attacks have similarly been directed against the military like in 1999 when NATO computers were hit by hactivists who protested NATO bombings in Kosovo.

c) **IP Address Spoofing**: This is a method that creates Transmission Control Protocol/Internet Protocol (TCP/IP) packets using somebody else's IP address. Routers use the "destination IP" address to forward packets through the Internet but ignore the "source IP" address and that is capitalized on in DDOS attacks to hide the true identity of an attacker.

d) **Sniffer**: Although sniffer programs are used for legitimate network management function like monitoring data traveling over a network, they are also deployed in cyber-attacks for stealing information including passwords off a network. Sniffers could be inserted almost anywhere through different means and once emplaced, they are very difficult to detect.

e) **Physical Attacks**: This involves actual physical destruction of a computer system and/or network – terminal equipment as well as wired or cyber traffic networks.

2.2 ATTACKS PECULIAR TO ALL TARGETS

Without exemption, every computerized device user risks the following attacks:

1. **E-mail Spoofing** - E-mail spoofing is faking an e-mail as originating from a source different from the actual sender. The aim is to trick the recipient into taking decisive actions or releasing sensitive information (such as passwords). For instance, cyber criminals often send emails purportedly from national or world bodies requesting awardee(s) to send sensitive information for direct crediting of their bank accounts.

2. **Keylogger** - A software or hardware used for monitoring and logging keys that a user is punching on a computer keyboard. The key-log is later reviewed by whosoever installed the monitoring device with view to extracting passwords and other sensitive information a target is legitimately shielding from public view.

3. **Logic Bomb** – This program destroys data by reformatting a hard disk or randomly inserting garbage into data files. It infects a computer via a downloaded program from a compromised public-domain. Once a logic bomb is executed, it wreaks havoc immediately unlike other viruses that destroys gradually.

4. **Viruses** - A computer virus is a malicious software that spreads by first infecting files or the operating system of a computer or the hard drive of a network router before multiplying itself. Most viruses cause harm by damaging data and system files.

   Unlike in the past when viruses were spread through sharing of portable storage media like disks, viruses are now spread mostly through email messages. It takes a victim's action such as opening an email attachment or visiting a malicious website for a computer to get infected by a virus. There are different types of viruses including:

- **Boot Sector Virus** - Initially infects a few sectors of a computer's hard drive or disk for the virus to activate as the drive or disk boots.

- **Companion Virus** - Stores itself in a file similar in name to a program file that is commonly executed. When that file is executed the virus infects the computer and/or performs malicious steps including deleting entire content of a hard disk drive.

- **Executable Virus**: This stores itself in an executable file and infects other files each time the infected file is run. Generally, that is how computer viruses are spread – by opening or executing an infected file.

- **Overwrite Virus**: Overwrites a file with its own code for a viral spread to other files and computers.

- **Polymorphic Virus**: This virus is capable of changing its own code for hundreds or thousands of different variants - making it very difficult to notice or detect.

- **Resident Virus**: Stores itself within a memory to infect files instantaneously without a target having to inadvertently execute a command.

- **Stealth Virus**: Hides its tracks by purporting that no part of a memory or file size has altered after infecting a computer with modifications.

5. **Zombie** - A computer or server that has been basically hijacked by a hacker using some malicious software to perform a Distributed Denial of Service (DDOS) attack.

6. **Worm** - A worm is a virus variant that spreads from computer to computer without a victim's interaction. Starting with just a computer, a

worm finds and infects other computers because it propagates via email, websites, or network-based software. Worms pave way for remote access and attacks by criminals besides hampering the normal functioning of a computer.

7. **Trojan horse** - A Trojan horse is a software that purports to perform a positive function while actually doing something sinister behind the scenes. Once inadvertently installed, it performs a criminal function in the background such as allowing other users to have access to your computer or automatically sending information from your computer to other computers.

   For instance, "free" anti-virus software claiming to protect your computer could actually be exporting sensitive data to an intruder. Trojan horses come disguised in "free" software download offers or email attachments.

8. **Spyware** - This software has both legitimate and criminal uses. While marketers use it to gather consumer data for advertising, criminals deploy extremely invasive versions to capture information on email addresses, screenshots, keystrokes, authentication credentials, web form data, browsing habits and any other personal information to facilitate crime.

   Targets are vulnerable as they visit a malicious website or one that uses no data encryption (see the section on data protection by encryption).

The foregoing are the illegal ways by which criminals could gain access to a target's information to facilitate crime. The sections that follow centre on how to organize your defence to counter their onslaught.

Chapter 3

INTERNET CONNECTIVITY AND SECURITY ISSUES

The capacity of the Internet as a one-stop source for intelligence gathering holds a big promise for criminals. That is why they are ever researching for more areas of vulnerability to exploit. Therefore, any attempt at mitigating cyber threats must first of all consider the different facets of the Internet that could render a target vulnerable.

To that end, the following aspects: mode of internet connectivity; choice of internet service provider; integrity of a website and website certificate; choice of a web browser; secure browsing and; managing email accounts would now be examined.

3.1 MODES OF CONNECTIVITY

There are two modes, namely dial-up and wireless either of which could be used for connecting to the Internet. This distinction is important because either mode of connectivity has security implications as follows:

3.1.1 Dial-Up or Wired Internet Access - This is also known as "dial-on-demand" service and the traditional mode of Internet access. By this, a computer is connected to the Internet only when there is need - an email is to be sent or browsing is to be done. The connection is thereafter disconnected manually or automatically after some idle time elapses.

Its security advantage lies in your computer being dynamically assigned a different IP address with every request for Internet access. That makes it difficult, if not impossible for an attacker to take control of your computer via a vulnerable network service.

n comparison, a typical wireless or broadband service referred to as "always-on" service is by far more vulnerable.

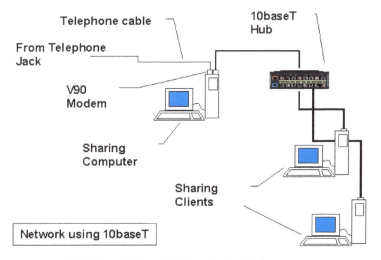

Dial-Up or Wired Internet Access sketch
Diagram credit: www.practicallynetworked.com

Computers on broadband networks are always on and ready to send or receive data through their network interface card (NIC). The inherent security risk arises because the connection is always on and with your computer's IP address hardly altering; it is more or less a fixed target for attack.

Even though attackers may initially not pin-point your computer, they would be able to identify the service range of your ISP because broadband service providers' IP addresses for home users are public knowledge. There lies the heightened risk of attack on a target using a broadband network.

However, the choice of a mode of connectivity largely depends on what is available in your environment. Wireless or broadband internet access through cable, DSL or fiber optic is more popular because it is virtual and inevitable where wired or dial-up access is out of reach.

18

3.1.2 Wireless Access or Connectivity and Mitigating Inherent Security Threats - As the name suggests, wireless networks or Wi Fi make virtual connection to the internet possible without visible wires. Wireless networks depend on radio waves and not cables to connect computing devices to the internet. A transmitter enabling wireless access point or gateway is wired into an internet connection to provide a "hotspot" for internet connectivity over radio waves.

A wireless Internet Access or Connectivity sketch
Diagram credit: jlwatsonconsulting.typepad.com

Through identifying information and an item known as SSID (service set identifier), hotspots are located by computing devices with wireless card and access permission. While, some computers can automatically identify open wireless networks in a given area, it follows that for others, a hotspot has to be located and SSID information manually entered for network access.

In effect, with wireless connectivity, you can access an ISP's network from anywhere - home, office, airport, etc. that is within radio coverage.

However, the potential of mobile computing which is popularizing the adoption of wireless connectivity is fraught with peculiar risks as a wireless network infrastructure is more exposed and therefore, insecure compared to wired circuits. The virtual nature of wireless networks requiring no wire

19

between a computing device and an internet connection makes it possible for attackers who are within range to hijack or intercept an unprotected connection.

The crime known as wardriving entails anyone armed with a computer, a wireless card and a GPS device, driving through an environment to search and identify the coordinates of a wireless network location or service provider.

The information gathered in that manner is usually posted online for those with vested interest in the wardriving to use for hijacking a wireless network or intercepting the connection between your device and a hotspot.

By implication, Internet enabled portable devices like laptops, smartphones and tablets are at risk. That would be especially so where protection for home and office wireless networks or computing devices is either scanty or utterly lacking owing to reliance on assumed protection by network service providers.

Also, because a "Wi-Fi" network for home use does not require account numbers and are always "on" as a wireless network, with a scanner on the Wi-Fi protocol, an attacker can monitor such a network for the chirping of a cell phone, computer or tablet to download its traffic or files. And as those devices are most vulnerable when in a "discoverable" or "visible" mode, it is advisable to turn off both the Wi-Fi and Bluetooth features when not needed.

Another concern is that during transmission, a wireless device could reveal a user's location to within a few metres because the transmission as well as the "cell" carrying it can be traced. Thus a criminal who happens to have stolen a list of customers from a carrier could locate or identify target(s) from transmissions.

Therefore:

- If Wi-Fi is integral to your cell phone, mouse, keyboard, laptop, etc., configure your device(s) not to discover new connections or otherwise, to alert you. Similarly, when not expected, receive no files transmitted over Wi-Fi/Bluetooth channels.

- When not in use, it is best to turn off both the Wi-Fi and Bluetooth features of your device.

- Change default passwords of network devices like wireless access points which come pre-configured with default administrator passwords meant to facilitate setup. That is critical because clues to default passwords are easily found online, thus constituting a security risk. Changing default passwords would make it difficult for criminals to take control of a device.

- Specifically, replace the local administrator password on a wireless access port with yours; disable remote administrator access; run current firmware and security software; and your name, address, or other identification details should not show in the new defaults. Effect the changes yourself if a vendor would not as otherwise your network could be exposed to eavesdropping and manipulation.

- Restrict access by allowing only authorized users to access your network. This can be achieved because every hardware seeking connection to a network has a MAC (media access control) address and by filtering MAC addresses, you can restrict or allow access to your network.

Information on how to enable technology features that mandate wireless devices to authenticate themselves before accessing a network is found in accompanying users' guides.

- Encrypt the data on your network so that in a worst case scenario, anyone who hacks into your network will not be able to view your data. For this purpose, there are two separate programs namely WEP (Wired Equivalent Privacy) and WPA (WiFi Protected Access) either of which could be used to encrypt information in a wireless device. However, WPA gives better security than WEP.

- Protect the Service Set Identity (SSID) of your wireless router by asking the vendor at purchase to change the default to one unique to you and difficult to guess by attackers. Also, the SSID broadcast should be disabled. If a vendor would not take these steps for you, follow instructions in your user guide and effect the necessary changes.

  Otherwise, your network could be exposed to eavesdropping and manipulation.

- For an added layer of protection, install a firewall (client based) directly on your wireless device(s) to preempt attackers who might be able to circumvent your network firewall. This is even more important because the wireless network in a building might lack the protection.

  Meanwhile, in addition to installing the appropriate firewall variant for a computer or a handheld device, other measures including data encryption (already mentioned above) should be taken for greater security and privacy.

- Install and update anti-virus software to minimize any damage attackers might be able to inflict on your network and wireless computing device(s). Hybrids that equally protect against spyware and Trojan horses should be preferred.

- Screen message contents to forestall giving criminals clues to sensitive information and do not store authentication codes like passwords and PINs in your mobile computing device(s).

This is important because communicating over wireless networks is like broadcasting to the world besides portable devices standing a high risk of being stolen or lost.

3.2 CHOICE OF INTERNET SERVICE PROVIDER

An Internet Service Provider (ISP) is an organization that maintains a direct Internet link to give clients access for web browsing and email communications via a supplied software interface, a pass-worded user account, and an electronic standard (e.g. modem) for connecting to the internet.

The modem, especially the wireless model is supplied by many ISPs as part of service contract for customers to use Wi Fi equipped wireless devices to access the Internet.

Also, some ISPs render website construction and hosting services to customers who desire to maintain personal web pages. Again, some ISPs double as telecommunication services providers. Because the choice of an ISP has security implications, the following selection criteria should be considered:

- Security should not be sacrificed for quality services and competitive prices although both are important. Therefore, ascertain whether your potential ISP uses both encryption and secure socket layer (SSL) to protect submitted information (e.g., user name, password, etc.).

  Similarly, if a wireless modem is provided, find out the level of wireless security standards supported besides their compatibility with your computing devices?

- An ideal ISP should be capable of verifying the identities or sources of emails to block Spam, junk or unsolicited mails from entering your computing device and diverting those with unidentified addresses to a store for review. An ISP should implement firewalls for blocking that

23

portion of incoming traffic even though supplementary to your own system's firewall.

- Privacy policy and recommendations concerning a prospective ISP should be accessed for acceptability or otherwise. With respect to privacy in particular, you should be satisfied as to who has access to your information and the possible uses. Also, reviews on an ISP from trusted sources should inform your decision.

- Backups of email and web files are important to recovery from cyber attacks and if that is critical for you, confirm that an ISP offers the service because it is normally not advertised.

- Ability of an ISP to maintain required security standards could be influenced by its ownership and organizational structure. For instance, some are operated by single individuals and others, by large corporations.

  Also, in terms of coverage or scope, some serve only patrons in a city while others have national, regional or international spread. Naturally, an ISP with public ownership and elaborate organizational structure would offer more reliable services.

3.3 WEBSITE CERTIFICATION AND INTEGRITY

Organizations or corporations that care about the security of those that visit or supply information on their website, maintain a data encryption capability evidenced by a site or host certificate.

So, you owe yourself a duty to confirm that a website is certified by trusted third parties as capable of securing your sensitive information online by encryption. That could be at a glance by ascertaining presence of two tokens thus:

- a closed padlock, which may be located on the status bar at the bottom of your browser or at the top between the address and search fields and;

- a URL (explained below) beginning with "https:" and not "http:"

A URL beginning with "https:" rather than "http:" confirms data protection.
Graphic credit: hallaminternet.com

Meanwhile, URL standing for Uniform Resource Locator is unique to a web page as an address by which a computing device finds a web page. An example is: https://braingain.com/index.html.

3.3.1 Website Certificate: Relevance - A website certificate attests that a certification authority has duly authenticated a website as actually belonging to a legal entity. That is to forestall unknowingly patronizing websites or cloned versions of popular organizations operated by criminals. In fact, apart from the credibility of the owner, how much you trust a website should depend on the track record of the certification authority.

Therefore, before submitting any sensitive information on a website, you should be satisfied with the credibility of the certification authority. To that end, every browser holds by default, a list of more than 100 trusted certification authorities.

The implication is that you have to confirm any one of those certification authorities as having properly verified and validated an organization's identity or the authenticity of its website. While the most trusted certification authorities include VeriSign, thawte, Entrust, etc., always confirm that an issuing authority is genuine and trusted.

Even with an assurance of data protection, read an organization's privacy policy for a feel of what would be done with your information before you comply. However, after exercising your option to examine a certificate, you may accept the certificate forever, for that particular website visit or not at all.

3.3.2 Website Certificate: Verification - Specifically, verification of a website certificate could be done in either of two ways on Internet Explorer or Firefox web browsers. One way is to click on a padlock icon on either browser.

However, for security reasons you might not find every browser's settings configured to display the status bar that has the padlock icon because criminals could fake the icon to display a false dialog window when clicked upon. Therefore, it is safer to use the other method of authenticating a website certificate which involves searching for the certificate token in the menu options.

Basically, ownership names on both a website and its certificate must tally just as its validity period must not be longer than two years. Normally, details attesting a certification authority, organization to whom a certificate has been issued and an expiration date, are displayed via a dialog box after simply typing an URL or following a link.

As a feedback, your browser would confirm whether a website address matches the address on a certificate and if the certificate is signed by a certification authority recognized by the browser as a "trusted" authority.

Meanwhile, a dialog box claiming that there is an error with a website certificate would pop-up, if your browser senses a problem. And it could be that the name on the certificate does not match the website name; that you previously chose not to trust the certificate issuing company or; that the certificate has expired.

At other times, the confusion might have arisen because the certificate was issued to a department and not an organization as a corporate body.

Chapter 4

WEB BROWSERS AND SECURE BROWSING

A web browser as a program or software that searches and displays web pages, interfaces between your computing device and a web server or computer hosting a website of your interest. Web browsers make possible, navigation or roaming of the internet - the world-wide-web (www) and there is a variety of web browsers to suit different needs.

However, the most popular are graphical browsers that display text and graphics with some capable of multimedia functions (text, audio and video). These include: Internet Explorer, Firefox, Opera, Safari (specific to Apple Inc. products), Lynx (text-based and for vision-impaired users), etc.

At least, one browser is usually embedded in the operating system of a computer and you can always replace or supplement it with more for the level of security you desire. However, with more browsers on the same device, you will be prompted to select one as your default browser for automatically opening web pages and emails when you double click links.

4.1   BROWSER RISKS

When any browser is opened and a web address (URL) for a website is typed in, the browser sends a request to a server or servers that are to supply the required content. In response, the server(s) sends a code written in a language such as HTML, JavaScript, or XML which the browser then processes but with implications for security owing to:

1. **Active Contents** - To enhance functionality or embellish designs, website construction or constitution depends on scripts like JavaScript, VBScript, ECMAScript, and JScript to execute programs within web browsers. Those scripts otherwise known as active contents are used to

27

create "splash pages" or options like drop-down menus.

Unfortunately, scripts or active contents are often used as conduits by criminals to download or execute malicious code on their targets' computing devices.

In particular, JavaScript combination with other software in website construction, fascinates criminals who manipulate it for attacks via unauthorized routing of users from legitimate websites to malicious ones for virus infection or intelligence gathering via spyware.

Unlike JavaScript and others used in websites for design embellishments, Java, Flash and ActiveX controls are programs that reside in your computer or downloadable online into a computing device to aid in formatting and displaying requested web pages.

Yet, at attackers' behest, ActiveX controls in particular, could do anything on your computer just like you, including running spyware to collect sensitive information or connecting to other computers at risk of harm.

2. **Cookies** – Similarly, with cookies as information about your browsing habits collected and stored in your browser, you could be vulnerable. The information might be as general as your IP address, the domain you use for connecting (e.g., .edu, .com, .net), browser type used or more specific information pertaining to your browsing habits like periods of web visits, personal preferences, etc.

Again, cookies could be sessional cookies that indicate web pages already visited during a session or persistent cookies - information about your personal preferences within specified time intervals.

3. All those details including your email address(es) or personalized home page that appears with every visit to any favorite website are stored in a web browser. The risk is that with illegal access to a computing device, an attacker could use cookies like authentication, preferences and other types of user information to track a user across multiple web sites.

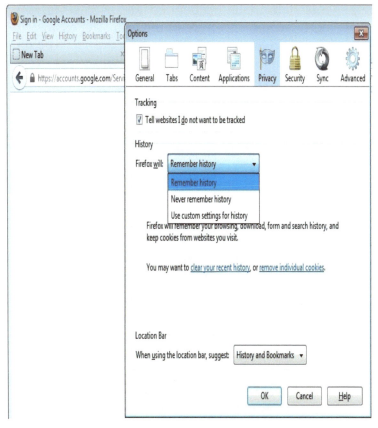

As active contents and cookies could be used as common tools for building profiles of individuals for attacks, do your privacy settings as appropriate.
Graphic credit: Microsoft Inc.

4. And by using correlation and techniques such as "web bugs" over time, cookies could be used to build profiles of individuals to facilitate attacks.

4.2   SECURE BROWSING

So, although not inherently risky, active contents and cookies as potential tools for attacks by criminals, pose hidden risks when viewed in browsers and email clients. Hence on the page after this would be found tested mitigation measures.

4.2.1 Varying Browser Security Settings - Every browser has default or predefined security settings that you can adjust and readjust as necessary for your security. Therefore, depending on the type of network - whether Home Network, Workplace Network or Public Network (Internet Café) at any given time, always search and adjust to the most appropriate security level (low, medium or high).

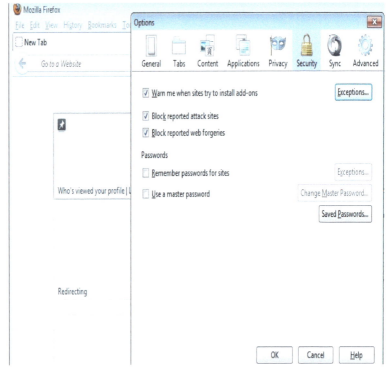

Based on the type of network whether Home Network, Workplace Network or Public Network (Internet Café) at any given time, always search and apply appropriate security settings.   **Pic credit**: Microsoft Inc.

While raising your security level would prevent you from being attacked, it could hamper some web pages loading or functioning properly. The best approach, therefore, is to adopt the highest level of security and enable certain browser features only when you require their functionality.

Similarly, because default options on certain browsers are for convenience and not security, any option that could allow a website to remember your password should be avoided. Otherwise, your sensitive information would be at risk in the event of a criminal attack on that website.

Even on social networks with the primary purpose of information sharing, you can still restrict access to some personal information by tinkering with your browser security settings.

4.2.2 Following Links to Unfamiliar Websites - Before clicking on a link to an unfamiliar website, disable active content as a precautionary step. The same measure is imperative for emails which are safer to view in plain text instead of HTML. While disabling active content from running in most browsers would heighten security online that would limit functionality or degrade some features of visited websites.

Therefore, a user should know which browsers support certain features and the inherent risks. A sequential process for securing your web browser, would be found on your vendor's website or by making a direct contact if such information is not on their website.

4.2.3 Blocking or Limiting Cookies - Adjust your privacy and security settings to block or limit cookies in your web browser. To foreclose other sites collecting unauthorized sensitive personal information, you may allow cookies only by the website you are visiting while blocking or limiting third-party cookies.

That is the more necessary when using a public computer and there is need to forestall criminals gaining access to your personal information.

4.2.4 Installation of Updates/Patches and Plug-ins - Prompt advantage should be taken of web browser updates or patches meant to address emergent security threats. Again, while there may be need to install ancillary software known as plug-ins such as Java and ActiveX controls, to enhance functionality of browsers, plug-ins may be used to facilitate attacks.

So, even with offers to download such software directly from vendors' websites, caution should be exercised to verify the credibility of a website.

4.2.5 Ascertain credibility of an organization and information protection capability - Before submitting sensitive information online, verify the site's privacy policy that states how any information supplied would be used and whether such information would be shared with some other organizations.

That is important because organizations sometimes share information with business associates or subsidiaries which is why you should watch against being added to mailing lists by default.

Therefore, before submitting sensitive information like your name, email address, or other personal information on a website, ascertain the site's privacy policy. If you cannot find any on a website, contact the company for clarification before submitting personal information. Or find a site offering better security. Privacy policy verification should be periodic because they sometimes change.

At all times, a website's capability to protect against criminal attacks and restrict access to only bonafide recipients of sensitive information should never be in doubt. An URL that begins with "https" as opposed to "http" and a lock icon at a corner of a web page indicate your information would be encrypted for protection.

The encryption must take care of the transit and storage phases respectively for all-round protection.

4.2.6 Excluding Debit Cards, devote one Credit Card to Online Purchases - With debit cards, charges for online purchases are deducted immediately and that is why any criminal access to your account data could empty your bank account within a short time. In comparison, with a ceiling on the monetary value you are liable to pay in the event of identity theft, credit cards give some protection.

However, to minimize possible losses in the event of a criminal access to your credit card information, you could open a credit card account purposely for online use. Also, a fixed amount of credit line would place a lid on how much a criminal could accumulate to your charge.

With a ceiling on extent of liability in the event of identity theft, credit cards hold an advantage over debit cards.
Pic credits: articles.bplans.com and handsonbanking.org

Meanwhile, frequently check your bank and credit card statements. If your account is compromised, you have sixty days to challenge any fraudulent charges by your credit card company on the strength of receipts and statements of account.

But for a debit card, you have only about two days to take up any suspicious activity with your service provider. So, instead of a debit card, a credit card is better because you have sixty days to dispute fraudulent charges before probably suffering loss.

4.2.7 Multiple Web Browsers - You could install different browsers on your computer for separate activities. That way, one browser could be dedicated to sensitive activities like online banking, e-commerce, emailing, etc. with others used for general purpose web browsing. Although this would require configuring several web browsers for your computer, it would minimize risking sensitive data to web browser or website vulnerability.

4.2.8 Reacting and Mitigating Fallouts of an Online Security Breach - Any inadvertent disclosure of sensitive corporate information should be reported promptly to relevant officials and network administrators within your organization. This would put them on notice to watch out for any unusual or suspicious activity. Also:

- Immediately, change any passwords that might have been compromised. The process should be carried out for each account if multiple accounts use the same password (never advisable).

- If you suspect that your sensitive information may have been compromised and your safety is at risk, consider notifying the police promptly.

- With a view to confirming any suspicion of criminal action resulting from identity theft, watch out for any unexplainable charges to your accounts. In the end, contact your financial institutions to close accounts that might have been compromised.

Chapter 5

EMAILS AND IMPLICATIONS FOR SECURITY

At least, one email client comes embedded in the operating system of every computer and a user could supplement that or choose from an array of alternatives. Apart from a major difference in user interface, an email client could be web-based or a stand-alone application installed directly in your computer. Nowadays, portable or wireless devices including cell phones and tablets have variants of email clients preloaded for use on the go.

Baring compatibility problem, a user can install more than one email client on a computer out of which one could be selected as a default account. This would enable your computer open the email client by default whenever you click an email link in a message or browser.

5.1 TYPES OF EMAIL ACCOUNTS

Meanwhile, an email client could be corporate/stand-alone or a free service.

5.1.1 Corporate and Stand-alone Email Accounts - Some ISP or workplace issued email accounts are stand-alone programs installed directly and accessed only through computers with distinct settings and special access privileges.

While mails in stand-alone email clients are accessible only by host computers, other email clients are web-based programs that are accessible from virtually anywhere. That does not necessarily mean they are the same as free email accounts like Yahoomail, Hotmail, Gmail, etc.

For security reasons, neither use corporate and task-specific email addresses for social networking nor have them listed in public directories. And except with official clearance, do not forward your official email address to a free email account.

Therefore, instead of submitting your official or primary email address for online shopping, requesting services or participating in online fora, you could deploy free email accounts.

5.1.2 Free Email Accounts - Yahoomail, Gmail, Hotmail, etc. are examples of free browser-based email accounts maintained directly by the vendors' servers and accessible from any computing device on the internet. Every free email service has a specific browser interface for granting access to patrons.

Free email services are particularly useful when your computer is not handy or you just relocated with no ISP. Even where it is possible to access your corporate email account via a cyber café or a shared wireless hotspot, security worries about exposing details of official or primary email account, makes a free email service ideal for non-sensitive communication.

Actually, the low points of free email services bother on privacy and security of users' sensitive information. Because users are not paying for the accounts, the vendors might not be strongly committed to offering high standard service or protecting a user from both privacy and security threats.

Therefore, numerous benefits apart, free email services should not be used to send sensitive information. No matter the kind of network, whether fixed or wireless, free email accounts are not secure. Particularly, unencrypted emails are vulnerable to identity theft, forgery, surveillance, routing to third parties and illegal content editing whether enroute or inside public servers.

5.2 CHOOSING AN EMAIL CLIENT: SECURITY AND PRIVACY CONSIDERATIONS - Although functionality, reliability, availability, ease of use and visual appeal are all factors to consider in settling for an email client, security should take ascendency over every other factor.

Therefore, any software you choose for your emails should guarantee secure communication between you and your correspondents. To that end, some factors to consider include:

5.2.1 Requisite Level of Security - The email program you opt for should guarantee the level of security desired for sending, receiving and reading emails. If the bulk of your information is sensitive, the email program should make it possible for messages to be digitally signed for proof of integrity and encrypted for protection.

At a glance, a closed padlock image located on the status bar of a browser window and an URL beginning with "https:" rather than "http:" should confirm whether an email program guarantees data encryption.

5.2.2 Deficiencies of home-brewed Email Software - Email programs developed in-house may not be as secure and reliable as those of professional software developers which are tested and actively maintained. Therefore, be wary of "home-brewed" email software.

5.2.3 Email Software Downloads - Although some vendors offer an option of downloading their email software directly from their websites, ascertain the authenticity of a website before downloading such files.

5.2.4 Attention to Privacy Policies - Because you are not paying for a free email account, the service provider may trade some of your information to offset costs of providing the service.

Therefore, take time to read a service provider's privacy policy or terms of use to ascertain if your name, email address, those of others in your address book or any of the information in your profile could find their way to other organizations.

Needless to advise that you should outrightly "unsubscribe" from an email service that is altogether silent about privacy policy.

5.2.5 Run Up-to-Date Software - Never delay to install software patches to preempt attackers taking advantage of known vulnerabilities of older applications. Such software include system, application and security (anti-virus, anti-spyware, firewalls, etc.) software. Whenever newer versions are available, enable your operating system and other software for automatic updates.

5.2.6 Decide on Creating separate User Accounts - With some operating systems, you can create multiple user accounts which could enable you read your email on an account with restricted privileges. This is vital because some viruses cannot infect a computer except with "administrator" privileges.

5.2.7 Minimize Risks at Cyber Cafés - If you must patronize a public computer or so-called cyber cafes to access a web-based email account for mails, ensure you disable the ''keep me signed or logged in" option before signing into your email box as otherwise, your email could still be opened after you have signed out and left.

Besides, it is easy for criminals to install key-loggers in cyber cafe computers to secretly record information of users. Also, software that record keystrokes, retain deleted messages and cached items might be hidden in those computers.

By implication, your login credentials could be uncovered and the sites you visited called up which is why you might not be allowed to close your browser when logging off. And that is why one should use public computers neither to handle sensitive transactions nor access official web-based email accounts.

Therefore, if possible, empty the computer trash bin, clear the Web browser cache and reboot the computer you used to clean out your login credentials and materials. Otherwise, immediately after patronizing a cyber café, consider your login credentials compromised and contact your ISP to change your password and account data.

5.3 CHOOSING AND PROTECTING PASSWORDS

Passwords are often the weakest link in a computing device's security because computers used for cracking passwords are getting more than ever powerful. For instance, network passwords that once took weeks to crack can now be cracked in hours.

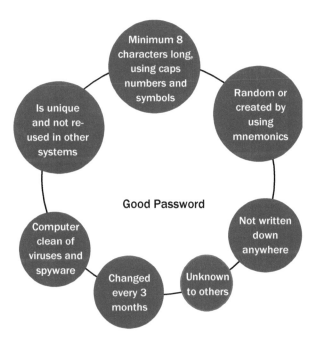

Failure to use good passwords and keep them secret would be nothing short of suicide. **Diagram credit:** Digital Security & Privacy for Human Rights Defenders

However, in the absence of more reliable alternatives, passwords are still the most common means of authenticating or ensuring that only authorized persons can access computerized information.

Therefore, failure to use good passwords and keep them secret would be nothing short of suicide. That explains why many systems and services are successfully infiltrated just as viruses and worms exploit other systems by guessing or cracking weak passwords. So, you must choose good passwords and keep them secret to make it difficult, if not impossible for criminals to access your information online.

Most passwords based on personal information or daily usage words are easy for criminals to crack or guess by "dictionary" attacks. This risk could be overcome by deliberately misspelling such words (as in "daytt" for date) and safer to use mnemonics. For example, "IITpfb" could stand for "(I) (l)ike (T)o (p)lay (f)oot(b)all.

Also, while a combination of lower and upper case letters would produce a good password, inclusion of numbers and special characters is even better (e.g. Il!3pFb).

Better still, for stronger passwords you could opt for passphrases which by their lengths are more secure and very difficult to guess. For example, "The phraseWD 4 my email!" would be a very strong password. However, popular phrases, quotations or song lyrics should be avoided while choices of passphrase must accord with limits imposed by the email service in use.

Also, to forestall collateral harm in the event of a successful criminal attack, each email account should have a separate password or passphrase.

Further, watch out for any attempt at tricking you to reveal your password which as well, should not be written anywhere it could be easily stolen. Always remember to log out after using a public or shared computer at your workplace.

Above all, patronize only internet service providers (ISPs) that use multiple means such as Kerberos, challenge/response or public key encryption to authenticate patrons as opposed to simple passwords.

5.4 SUPPLEMENTING PASSWORDS

Even though passphrases composed of symbols, numbers and mnemonics could serve as more reliable passwords, passwords as a layer of defence against cyber attacks are still vulnerable to being guessed or intercepted by attackers. So, as an additional security measure, it is better to maintain an email account with a service provider that has additional ways of verifying user identity.

For example, some organizations are now using a two-factor authentication, i.e. a password in conjunction with an extra piece of information. Because the second component is usually a "one use" password, an attacker who has managed to decode your primary password cannot proceed further without the second which is never valid for repetitive use.

An alternative to supplementing passwords is a certificate embedding all information required to identify a user. Like individuals examining certificates for website authentication, some websites verify user identity against personal web certificates in a public/private keys authentication system. Here, a password is not really needed because information identifying you is already embedded in a virtual certificate or key held by you.

But your private key must be password protected against attacks. Although similar to two-factor authentication, the difference lies in the fact that the password protecting your private key is meant only for decrypting information on your computer and is never sent over the network or online where it could be attacked.

Meanwhile, loss of personal web certificates stemming from reformatting of computers can be overcome by your service provider reissuing the certificate on request. Similarly, you could be reminded of a forgotten password through an identification process involving you successfully answering "secret question(s)" based on a questionnaire you initially completed to open an email account.

For answers to the "secret question(s)" to truly serve the purpose of supplementing your password, the opposites of personal information like mother's maiden name, date of birth, etc. should instead have been supplied to preempt attackers guessing the answers.

Besides email accounts, good password processes can similarly protect bank accounts, credit cards or other sensitive information stored in trust by organizations.

Therefore, choose good passwords and ensure they are secure from the reach of criminals. To that end, do not shy away from demanding to know the kind of security practices adopted by an organization to protect your information.

5.5   RELEVANCE OF BCC

BCC which stands for "blind carbon copy", enables you to hide addressees in an email message so that individual recipients cannot decipher who else received the same email.

While addresses in the **To** field and the **CC** (carbon copy) field would appear, addressees typed in the **BCC** field would not.

Among potential benefits of adopting BCC, security of individual recipients comes first before privacy, tracking, respect, information need and convenience. This is particularly important where there is need to keep individual email addresses confidential or where there is no need for recipients to know who else is receiving the same email. Otherwise, the criminally minded could take undue advantage to extract addresses for the purpose of committing crime.

Do not unduly expose others' email addresses and similarly, encourage them to forward messages to you as BCC to forestall your email address being harvested for crime.
Diagram credit: Digital Security & Privacy for Human Rights Defenders

While you should not unduly expose your contacts' email addresses, you can similarly encourage them to forward messages to you as BCC to forestall your email address appearing in other people's inboxes and being harvested for crime.

Finally, most email clients have the BCC option below the **To** field while it is a separate option not listed by default in others. So, you have to search for it by checking the help menu or the software's documentation. Further, except you type an address on the **To** field, your email client might not BCC your intended recipients. Therefore, you may have to put your own email address on that field.

5.6 ATTACHMENTS AND THE NEED FOR CAUTION

One of the features that make many email services user-friendly is ease of attaching and forwarding documents along with emails. While almost any type of file can be attached to an email message, some email clients have an option of automatic downloading of email attachments.

Unfortunately, criminals exploit those user friendly features as licence to email all types of viruses to targets – placing computers and entire networks at risk of viruses via attachments. However, as attachments would not harm except when opened, exercise caution at all times. Specifically, see to the following:

5.6.1 Unsolicited Attachments - Be wary of unsolicited attachments because emails may not actually emanate from the sources you suppose. So, it advisable to check with the supposed sender to ascertain its legitimacy before opening any attachments.

While it should be borne in mind that patches and email software do not come as attachments from vendors and ISPs respectively, every purported emails from those sources should be scrutinized like any other.

5.6.2 Don't Disobey Your Instincts - There might be a justification for your being uncomfortable about an email or the attachment. So, do not let curiosity carry the day and put your computing device at risk. Even if your anti-virus indicates that a mail is harmless, do not open an attachment directly because attackers are ever innovating with new viruses.

5.6.3 Before Opening Attachments, Save and Scan them - If you must open an attachment before being able to ascertain the source, be sure your anti-virus software are up to date. Yet, first save the file to your computer or a disk; manually scan the file and if the file is safe, then open it.

5.6.4 Disable Automatic Downloading of Attachments - Find out if your software enables automatic downloading of attachments and disable the option.

5.7 SIGNING YOUR EMAILS, IMPORTANT TERMS AND DIGITAL SIGNATURES - The ease with which criminals use viruses to "spoof" email addresses sometimes makes it difficult to determine legitimate emails. Yet, in official or business transactions, assurance of the integrity of correspondence is an imperative.

For example, anyone relying or expecting vital information from someone would like a token that the information did actually emanate from the right source without any malicious modification. Digital signatures are meant to satisfy that need.

Although there are different types, the focus here is on digital signatures for authenticating emails. A digital signature is a block of letters/numbers which comes last at the bottom of emails. The signature is generated by combining both key and a particular email's information - using a mathematical algorithm. The process leaves a random-looking string of letters and numbers.

Keys, key ring, fingerprint, key certificate and web of trust are fundamental to generating a digital signature. To append a digital signature, two keys – private and public are vital; the private version which you use to sign is verified against your public version already known to your correspondents. This authentication is possible because other correspondents like yourself would already have loaded the public versions of their keys into a public key ring – a server.

For ease of reference you can create a key ring of your own by downloading from a public key ring or by compiling a list with public keys your correspondents have sent to you.

Also, the uniqueness of the series of letters and numbers that form a digital signature is the fingerprint that is ascertained in every authentication. As for a key certificate, this is a collection of information such as the name of a key owner, the date it was created and when it would expire – all that show up when you select a key from a ring for verification.

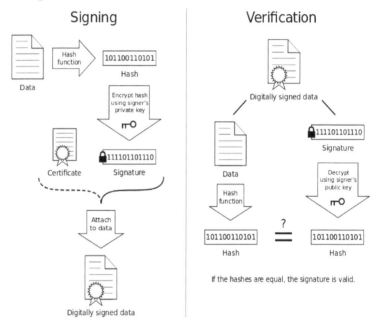

Digital signatures authenticate information as emanating from the sources claimed and appear last at the bottom of emails like random string of letters and numbers. **Sketch credit**: Google Inc.

Finally, the more your key is authenticated as yours by others, the more your "website of trust" grows with more people spurred to trust your key. However, never join a bandwagon yourself; always verify fingerprints yourself while keeping the password of your private key as top secret.

5.8   CREATING/OBTAINING AND USING A DIGITAL SIGNATURE - To own and use a Digital Signature, do the following:-

- Use software such as PGP, abbreviation for Pretty Good Privacy or GnuPG, meaning GNU Privacy Guard to generate a key.

- To heighten its authenticity, have your key signed or authenticated by co-workers or associates who have their own keys. By implication, they are confirming that the fingerprint on the key you sent to them belongs to you. This authentication of your identity would boost trust in your key.

- Your signed or authenticated key should be loaded into a public key ring for anyone who receives an email from you to be able to verify the digital signature on it.

- As most email clients are capable of readily appending your digital signature, always sign your outgoing emails.

Meanwhile, it should be noted that there are other mechanisms for creating and indicating digital signatures. For example, S/MIME as one of those other mechanisms does not leave a fingerprint of a visible block of letters and numbers on an email and, the digital signature is verified indirectly by relying on a certification authority instead of directly with other users.   And proof that a signature has been verified may be an icon or note on an email.

Any error or doubt about a digital signature can be clarified by contacting the correspondent on phone or through a valid email address.

Chapter 6

GENERAL COMPUTING SECURITY

Already, the computer has been explicitly appraised as the nerve centre or operating system of the modern society. And its ubiquity in every sphere of human endeavour is ever heightening with frontiers continually pushed by mobile cellular technology - the fastest growing technology ever. Hence an estimated global 4.6 billion portable computing devices as far back as 2009 besides computers on fixed or wired internet connectivity. The ever rising computer dependency exposes new vulnerabilities which the criminally minded find irresistible.

Vulnerabilities occasioned by unforeseen imperfections in operating and application software render any piece of computing device vulnerable to criminal attacks. That hacking risk apart, the portability of computing devices like cell phones, tablets and laptops risks outright theft for intelligence to attack targets.

Also, beyond individual vulnerability, sensitive corporate information or client accounts are at risk in most attacks. Hence organizations panic when their computer networks are attacked or equipment stolen altogether. Even where there is no sensitive corporate information other than your own passwords, email addresses, telephone numbers, information on online accounts, etc., a lost or infiltrated computing device always give cause for concern.

Therefore, effective computing security should centre on preventing, detecting, and responding to attacks.

6.1   PHYSICAL SECURITY

These days the computing devices of choice are laptops, tablets and cell phones because of their portability and ease of wireless connection to the Internet or use for audio communication. Unfortunately, the same advantages of convenience and ease of connectivity endanger them to criminal

48

exploitation like being hacked or stolen for sensitive information.

Effective physical security is imperative as the portability hallmark of modern computing devices risks outright theft and exploitation for sensitive information.

Diagram credit: Digital Security & Privacy for Human Rights Defenders

The following are some ways to protect your device against information hacking and outright theft:

6.1.1 When away from your computer, lock it - For the criminally minded, a few minutes is enough time to successfully fiddle with your computer. So, when not in use or you are stepping aside for some time, lock your computer to foreclose unauthorized access for any reasons. This should ensure that it cannot be opened except the right password is logged in.

If you are a regular traveler and within densely populated areas, it is advisable to secure your laptop bag with an alarm or a lock for securing your device in a suitable furniture. Both security fixtures are off the shelf products that can be readily acquired.

6.1.2 Except when needed, disconnect Internet connection - Unlike dial-up or fixed line Internet access, broadband connections like DSL and Wi Fi always keep computer devices online with the risk of being harmed by attackers or viruses scanning your local area network targets.

For security reasons, therefore, disconnect from a broadband connectivity when there is nothing to do online. And at all times, enable your device's firewall protection to supplement that of your local area network.

6.1.3 Secure your mobile devices during travel(s) - Many computer users, especially those who travel for business, rely on laptops and personal internet-enabled devices like smartphones and tablets because they are portable and easily transported. But while those characteristics make them popular and convenient, they also make them ideal targets for thieves.

The hustle and bustle associated with public functions like conferences/conventions, trade shows, seminars, etc. give criminals cover to target choice infotech devices containing sensitive information. So, during trips, carry your portable device(s) about with you. If you are attending a conference or trade show, be especially wary - such events offer thieves a wide selection of portable devices that are likely to contain sensitive information.

Meal times as well as conference sessions are optimum times for thieves to check hotel rooms for unattended devices.

Generally, strive to secure your mobile devices for protection of both the gadgets and the information they hold. Therefore, prior to an overseas or extensive travel, clear your smartphone or other portable devices of non-essential personal information including drug prescriptions, old memos, business cards, expired documents, etc. as a criminal could use such information to piece your identity together for a crime.

Also, there is no need to show-off how InfoTech savvy you are in full glare of lurking thieves; otherwise, they will soon be on your trail. So, apart from seldom use of your device in the public, practice security by obscurity – carry your gadgets in non-traditional cases.

If you must use your mobile device in the public, ensure no one is seeing any sensitive information on your screen or passwords being typed.
Pic credit: www.cbc.ca

However, if you must use your laptop or mobile device in a public area, pay attention to people around you. Take precautions to shield yourself from "shoulder surfers" - make sure that no one can see you type your passwords or see any sensitive information on your screen.

6.1.4 Wi-Fi and Bluetooth connectivity in the public - Avoid using open Wi-Fi networks to conduct sensitive business transactions like banking and online shopping. Using Wi-Fi networks at places like airports, coffee shops and other public places is vulnerable to attackers intercepting any sensitive information used in your online transaction.

Therefore, if you must, for instance check your bank balance or make an online purchase while you are traveling, turn off your device's Wi-Fi connection and instead use your mobile device's cellular data for internet connection and not an unsecure public Wi-Fi network.

Using Wi-Fi networks at public places is vulnerable to attackers intercepting any sensitive information used in your online transaction. **Pic credit**.www.boxtutorials.com

Similarly, when not being used with earpieces for hands-free talking and external keyboards for easy typing, turn off Bluetooth connection on your phone. Otherwise, if the Bluetooth connection is open and you are not using your phone, cyber criminals could pair with it to steal sensitive information.

6.1.5 Charging your mobile devices in the public - Avoid connecting your mobile device to any computer or charging station at say, airport terminal or a shared computer over which you have no control. You risk a malicious computer gaining access to your sensitive data or installing malware if your mobile device is connected to a computer via a USB cable.

6.1.6 Protection against power fluctuations - Criminal threats apart, natural or technological factors can deprive you of your device and data. Although good safety habits and use of uninterrupted power supply systems can considerably minimize power supply related risks, consider shutting down altogether during a lightning storm or construction works likely to raise the odds of dangerous power surges.

6.1.7 If the device is lost - Loss or theft of a computing device should be reported immediately to appropriate authorities like law enforcement agencies, hotel, conference staff and your organization especially if sensitive corporate information are at risk; that will ensure they act quickly to curtail any possible damage.

6.1.8 Install tracking software. – Your mobile or portable devices should have lock, locate or wipe software to track and facilitate recovery when lost or stolen.

6.2 DATA SECURITY

Defence-in-depth or multi-layered security arrangements are the ultimate for securing sensitive areas, facilities or equipment and this is deservedly so for ICT infrastructure which as the hub of modern existence is of strategic importance to criminals. So, apart from the physical, there is need to add another security layer to protect data.

Data protection will ensure that even if your device is stolen or attacked on the Internet, probable loss of information would not result in serious consequences. To that end:

6.2.1 Optimize usage of passwords - As most computing devices butt, there are multiple prompts for passwords at various stages of the process. Those stages of the butting process should be passworded for data security.

While separate passwords should be created for different programmes, they should not be such that could easily be guessed by criminals just as options that allow your computer to remember your passwords should be discarded. Similarly, advantage should be taken of any additional means of authenticating authorized use or users.

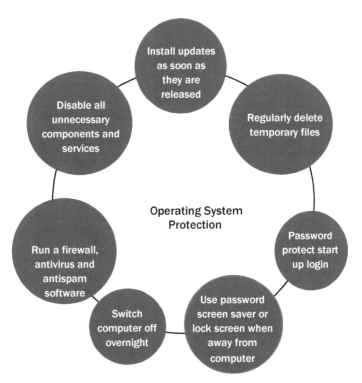

Periodically, upgrade the security features of your ICT devices to guard or secure your communications.

Diagram credit: Digital Security & Privacy for Human Rights Defenders

6.2.2 Preserve important data and back up your files - Whether by natural, technical or criminal causes, losing your data is awful. To forestall that risk, be proactive; regularly back-up your data onto network, CDs, DVDs, USB drives or thumb drives and keep them away at separate locations excluding your laptop bag.

That way, you will forestall losing important or all information as well as determine and report on any exact or important information that is at risk. Of course, how often you have to do your back-ups obviously depends on how constantly you update your data. In that case, it might be daily, weekly, monthly or once in a very long while.

6.2.3 Evaluate your Software and Security Settings - Most times computing devices are sourced with the default settings of their software enabling every available functionality. Although that offers an optimal browsing or online experience, it is fraught with risks.

So, as most software, especially browsers and email programs offer a variety of options, tinker with those settings to accord with your security needs. This precaution should be observed when a patch or a new version of a software is installed. As would be recalled, more and specific information on browser security were earlier supplied in this same chapter.

6.2.4 Uninstall redundant software or programs - Almost by default, software in regular use get patched or updated against emergent vulnerabilities more than those lying dormant and therefore, rendering the entire device vulnerable to attacks. So, it is advisable to uninstall software or programs cluttering your computer.

6.2.5 Guidelines for computer use and different user accounts - When different people including children use the same computer, the risk of someone accidentally modifying, deleting or exposing your data to criminal exploitation is high.

To forestall that happening, set boundaries to regulate multiple access. This could be done by creating accounts for separate access and privileges for different users. Also, this separation could be for protective boundary between official work and personal data.

The option of separate user accounts is possible with most operating systems like Windows XP and Vista, Mac OS X, Linux, etc. Better still, separate computers could be set aside for official and personal uses respectively.

6.2.6 Encrypt sensitive files and acquire a Digital Certificate - Passwords and other security measures offer a degree of data protection but data encryption guarantees against unauthorized people viewing the content of a violated device.

Encryption protects a message or information by coding and it is particularly important for sending sensitive information which only an authorized person with a genuine key can decode. Otherwise, the message would remain a random series of letters, numbers, and characters and that is important because email messages could be intercepted online by attackers.

To encrypt a mail, find out the public key of the intended recipient or addressee from a public key ring. Next, confirm directly from the individual or organization that the series of letters and numbers associated with the key is their genuine fingerprint. If the response is in the affirmative, encrypt the email message using their public key by a feature in many email clients. On receipt, the recipient would decrypt it for access.

Further information on encryption and decryption of sensitive data would be found under digital signatures already discussed in this chapter. Meanwhile, bear in mind that it could cost money to acquire encryption capability and that prices are in proportion to the strength of protection offered.

For instance, a 56-bit system would checkmate casual hackers while a 128-bit program provides stronger security. Vendors include www.PGP.com and www.VeriSign.com among others, some of whom offer the program for free.

Also, for anyone not technically inclined, vendors do help to set up the program. Of the two available versions, GnuPG or GPG (GNU Privacy Guard) is available for free while the other, PGP (Pretty Good Privacy) which is preferred by most patrons is not free of charge.

Apart from encrypting individual emails or transmission of sensitive data, the entire website of an organization could adopt encryption to guarantee security of information submitted online. In technical terms that means acquiring a digital/site/host certificate or a computer ID card. This is important as those who submit sensitive data online would want assurance that such information would not end up at criminal websites.

Again, to ascertain if a website has a valid certificate and encrypts your information, watch out for a symbol of a closed padlock, which could be located at the bottom or top of your browser window between the search fields and address and/or; for URL that begins with "https:" rather than "http:". Meanwhile, you could acquire a free digital certificate from www.Thawte.com,

Finally, you may also consider full disk encryption to prevent unauthorized starting of your laptop. This encryption requires remembering passwords and passphrases to access a device. So, forgetting or failing to note such critical codes like passwords and encryption keys on paper hidden in a locked container could result in information loss.

6.2.7 **Stick to corporate guidelines for storing official information** - Official policies on information handling are meant to forestall unauthorized criminal access as well as immune organizations and their personnel against legal liability. Therefore, there should be implicit compliance. Even where such policies are merely implied, third parties should have no access to computing devices holding corporate data.

6.2.8 Patches and the Imperative of Updating your Software - Whatever anti-virus and firewall protection you have today might not be adequate tomorrow because hackers are always on the prowl to explore and exploit vulnerabilities. And in response, vendors promptly release upgraded versions or issue patches to fix discovered flaws. Once available, vendors usually put upgrades on their websites for users to download.

It is important to install a patch as soon as possible to protect your computer from attackers who are fast to take advantage of any known vulnerability.

In some cases, software would automatically search for updates online while some vendors offer users the option of automatic notifications of updates. Whatever the case, regularly visit your vendors' websites for such updates. As hackers might already be alert to your vulnerability, updates should be downloaded and installed promptly.

However, download software or patches from only trusted websites while avoiding email attachments or links that trick users to install viruses disguised as updates.

6.2.9 Install and Update Anti-virus Software for routine System Scanning - Anti-virus software detect and stop viruses from infecting your computing device. On the basis of already known patterns or signatures, anti-virus software scan files or an entire computer to detect virus infections. So, until vendors include new virus signature updates, you could be vulnerable to viruses presently out of the scope of your anti-virus.

There lies the limitations of anti-virus software and the very reason why updates should be sought regularly and installed as they are released by developers/vendors.

To that end, any offer of automatic updates by anti-virus developers/vendors should be accepted promptly. However, beware of email attachments purporting to be anti-virus software from the technical department of your ISP.

In fact, the attachment itself is most times a virus. For the same reason, resist any temptation to download free anti-virus software from the Internet. If need be, confirm any anti-virus information from your vendor or other vendors.

Depending on the software selected, it is possible to configure for automatic scanning of certain files or directories as well as prompting for periodic entire system scanning. Of course, files from outside sources should be manually scanned for any viruses. And as a precaution, email attachments and web downloads should, first and foremost, be saved into a hard disk before scanning. CDs and DVDs should similarly be scanned for viruses before being accessed.

Again, how the discovery of a virus is notified depends on the software and whether the scanning was automatic or manual. However, a virus would most times be displayed via a dialogue box giving you options, one of which is to "clean" or remove the virus.

Some other software attempt to remove the virus without your intervention. These and other differences dictate that you acquaint yourself on the features of your chosen anti-virus package. Finally, install anti-spyware discussed next if one is not already embedded in your anti-virus software.

6.2.10 Spyware Risks and Prevention:- Though very suggestive, the term "spyware" is not necessarily something used by secret or undercover agents. Rather, the term has more to do with the global advertising industry which is why it is also known as "adware." The ever expanding frontiers of e-commerce that has made internet the media of choice for advertising, accounts for the unbridled deployment of spyware or adware for intelligence gathering on consumer habits.

However, a spyware clandestinely installed on your device could capture information on email addresses, screenshots, keystrokes, authentication credentials, web form data, browsing habits and any other personal information; all without your consent. Most times, the data so collected are sold out to marketers or used by online attackers themselves to facilitate crime.

Therefore, once your computer begins to act like an electronic billboard displaying pop-up windows, redirecting you to websites other than the ones typed in your browser, displaying strange toolbars/icons, changing your browser or search engine, displaying random error messages, getting sluggish or certain keys stop responding (especially the Tab), safely conclude that a spyware is on the prowl.

Although seemingly harmless, the functioning of a spyware could constitute privacy violations depending on what information is being gathered, the destination and usage. Worse, criminals might use extreme invasive versions to build up intelligence for attacks just as the smooth functioning of a computing device could be jeopardized.

Therefore, if any troubleshooting confirms your suspicion of a spyware, use genuine anti-spyware application to scan your computer and remove all malware. Any anti-virus embodying anti-spyware software can also serve the purpose.

Generally, adhere to good security practices that serve both precautionary and recovery purposes including configuring your Anti-virus software to prompt on periodic full-scale system scanning.

Meanwhile, to forestall spyware installation on your device, do:

1. **Review End-User Licence Agreements before Software Installation** - End-User Licence Agreements (EULA) which appear most times like a dialog box, usually require users to accept contract conditions before software installation could proceed.

   Although an EULA is actually a contract between users and a software developer, the later sometimes take advantage of users' tendency of hurriedly accepting default "checked" options without actually considering the contractual implications.

   As legal contracts, EULAs may contain almost any conditions by developers and that is why original software as well as their updates or patches should be examined for any obnoxious terms. Apart from protecting the developer against liability or conferring right to install other software (updates or third party) on your computer, EULA may also contain other terms giving the vendor a degree of control over your device.

   That could translate to permitting the developer to monitor your computing activities for transmission of information back to the vendor or to some third parties which could have serious security and privacy implications depending on what information is being gathered.

   Most times, information regarding the vendor's right to install additional software or monitor operations is intentionally located near the end of data or concealed in lengthy paragraphs/fine print to make it difficult to detect. So, seemingly lengthy agreements or those hard to understand could serve as caution to reconsider installing a software.

Yet, many users hastily click 'next', 'next', 'next' to blindly accept default options in utter disregard of prompts and EULA terms. In the process, they inadvertently consent to the installation of adware or intrusive spyware in their computing devices.

Also, while it must be admitted that making information hard to locate online is difficult, software patrons bear ultimate responsibility for their actions. Therefore, before accepting an end-user license agreement, ensure you understand and are comfortable with the terms. Otherwise, you may be agreeing to conditions that you would later consider unfair because of unforeseen exposure to security risks.

2. **Recognize and Reject Fake Anti-Virus Offers -** Do not access pop-up windows and email links offering "free" anti-spyware and antivirus software. Often pop-up windows serve as the interface with spyware and if clicked or touched, installs spyware or other malware in a computing device.

Like invasive spyware, fake antivirus is designed to steal information from unsuspecting targets while mimicking genuine antivirus. In the same breath, such malware could do numerous system modifications that would make unauthorized operations difficult to stop or to uninstall the malicious software. The tell-tale signs of fake antivirus offers include pop-ups asking for sensitive information, flashing or displaying security warning signs before a target.

Fake anti-viruses and spyware are spread via search engines, emails, social networking sites and internet advertisements by criminals. And it is safer to shut a pop-up window by clicking the "X" icon on the title bar rather than the "close" link on the window which to the contrary might actually install the spyware it purports to close.

Generally, be cautious when following web links or opening attachments from unknown sources; keep software patched or updated and; visit vendors' websites to purchase or renew software subscription. On the whole, any Internet crime or fraud should be reported promptly to the appropriate law enforcement agency.

3. **Install and maintain Firewalls:–** Apparently, if anyone can remotely access your computing device via the Internet, you could be highly prone to attacks. However, any such probable criminal access can be forestalled by firewalls. Firewalls determine programs or applications in your computer that can interact on the Internet.

With two-way firewalls, incoming viruses can be stopped and any viruses already on-board a device, barred from unauthorized export of your data. Appropriately configured, firewalls would block cyber traffic emanating from specified locations while granting certain data right of way.

Firewalls are imperative for users whose computing devices are on "always on" Internet circuits like Wi Fi and DSL. In fact, it is wisdom for a computer without firewalls not to go online. Otherwise, it could send a thousand unauthorized emails on its own just as it would suffer a barrage of attacks within a short time. That risk would be greater where one is in transit and alternating networks for Internet access.

Although firewalls are offered in two separate forms, hardware (external) and software (internal), both could be combined for a layered two-way protection. The hardware version is an external or network firewall positioned between your computer and your cable or DSL modem.

Hardware firewalls come embedded in "routers" supplied by ISPs and other vendors with own operating systems that provide an additional layer of defence against attacks. And as hardware firewall is particularly meant for protecting computers on a network, your device may not need added software firewall protection, if other computers on your network can be adjudged free of viruses, worms and spyware.

However, software firewalls are in-built in some operating systems and require only enabling to compliment any external version. Otherwise, acquire a software firewall from reputable software vendors or ISPs. And except a website is reputable or secure, avoid risks inherent in Internet software downloads by safely installing your firewall from a CD or DVD.

Finally, both hard and software firewalls come with default configurations that a user could tinker with to achieve desired level of protection. Occasional alerts about current viruses or worms from your vendor or ISP could make that a routine just as they are ready to give you any technical assistance on request.

But while firewalls in conjunction with anti-virus software would forestall most attacks, do not indulge in a false sense of security by deliberately running suspect programs on your computer.

4. **Coordinate your Virus and Spyware Defence** - First and foremost, ascertain the compatibility and genuineness of the Anti-spyware and Anti-virus applications you plan to install in the same computing device.

While anti-virus and spyware software are both important for cyber security, a multiplicity of programs for the same task could be counter-productive to the smooth functioning of your system. Without doubt, that is why some vendors are now offering computer security software combining both anti-virus and anti-spyware capabilities.

However, if you must install separate programs, you will need just one each of anti-virus and anti-spyware programs. And in your investigation or research to select the very best, reckon with the amount of malware a security software recognizes and as well, how frequently updates are released.

Also, to ensure their compatibility with other software in your computer, it is advisable to install computer security software in phases for space to promptly address any compatibility issues.

Meanwhile, some genuine programs for scanning and removing spyware from computers include popular products like Lavasoft's Ad-Aware, Microsoft's Window Defender, Webroot's SpySweeper, Spybot Search and Destroy, etc. At least, a particular vendor is known to offer their brand for free while others sell theirs.

5. **Minimize risks of file sharing** - File sharing is facilitated by a technology that enables internet users to share files housed in their respective computing devices. Peer-to-peer (P2P) software that are used to share music files are the popular versions of file-sharing technology.

However, using P2P technology exposes users to risks like infection and attacks as the natural consequences of risking a device with sensitive information. While it is difficult to confirm file sources as trustworthy, P2P programs are often used by attackers to transmit malware like spyware, viruses, Trojan horses and worms as targets inadvertently download infected files into their computers.

Even where you are the one transferring files to some so-called trusted persons or organizations, criminals may be able to access sensitive personal or corporate information. And once information has been exposed to unauthorized people, the negative effect could be viral with heightened risk of identity theft and other forms of attack.

Therefore, the best way to escape inherent risks is to forego using P2P programs. But if you must use the technology, adhere to good security practices for risk reduction. To that end, install and keep your anti-virus software current.

Also, either install or enable firewalls because they can block some types of malware from entering your computer which is why you should not comply with any prompting by some P2P programs urging you to open certain ports on your firewall for file transmission. And the fact that there are some P2P applications that can modify and penetrate firewalls on their own, again reinforces avoidance as the best policy.

6. **Curb USB Drive Risks** - The triple advantages of portability, low prices and availability which make USB drives popular for storing and transporting data, similarly hold a strong appeal for criminals. When close enough, criminals use USB drives to physically steal information directly from computers. For example, there was panic with a USB stick containing Heathrow Airport's security plan, picked up on the street in October 2017.

A target's computer would be vulnerable even if it has been turned off. This is because even without power, a computer's memory remains active for several minutes within which an attacker could insert a USB drive, quickly reboot the system from the USB drive to copy sensitive data like passwords, encryption keys, etc. without a victim realizing.

Also, multiple computers could be attacked via USB drives that had deliberate contact with a computer for downloading malware into USB drives. Worse, depending on their stakes and clout, criminals can strike right at the manufacturing stage to infect USB drives destined for a particular market or high profile target(s).

Meanwhile, ease of theft and loss both constitute the most obvious security risk of USB drives as criminals could easily access information on drives that are not encrypted.

There are steps you can take to protect the data on your USB drive and in any computer you insert the drive. They are:

- **Adopt relevant security measures** - Use encryption and strong passwords on your USB drive to protect your data, create and keep backups away to insure against loss of your USB drive.

- **Don't Access unknown USB Drives and Keep separate USB Drives for Personal and Official Data** – Do not insert lost but found USB drives into your computer to either view the contents or decipher the owner. Instead, hand them over to the appropriate authorities like your organization's IT department or a location's security personnel.

  Neither access personal USB drives on workplace computers nor plug USB drives containing official information into personal computers.

- **Disable Autorun and Use Up-to-date Security Software** – An Autorun feature is reason why removable storage media like CDs, DVDs, and USB drives open automatically when inserted into a computer drive. Disabling Autorun in your computer's operating system will forestall a malware from an infected USB drive.

  Also, always use current firewall, anti-virus software and anti-spyware software to make your computer less vulnerable to attacks. As well, all your computer software should be updated or patched always.

- **Disposing data storage media properly** - It is usual of those discarding their old computer or throwing away a CD or DVD to copy out some useful files and trying to ensure no data is left behind for any unauthorized access. However, merely deleting a file does not actually erase it and except the process is appropriately carried out, hard drive, CD or DVD would still yield information for the criminally minded.

  For instance, even though difficult to locate, trash emptied out of your recycle bin is still somewhere in the system and an attacker could retrieve any sensitive information for malicious purposes. And that could border on identity theft negatively impacting you or affiliated organizations. Therefore, to forestall such a sad reality, ensure that sensitive files are effectively erased.

  As reformatting a hard drive, CD, or DVD might only superficially delete their information content, effectively overwriting the storage media with new content is the safer option. To that end, cautiously select both software and hardware devices meant for effectively erasing storage media based on the following criteria:

- **Perform "Secure Erase" multiple times** - Modern hard drives have a "Secure Erase" standard which by a command erases data by overwriting all areas of the hard drive. The overwriting process should be repeated three to seven times with a new layer of data each time to make it a near impossibility for an attacker to peel his way to success.

- **Use random data and zeros in the final layer** - Random data as opposed to easily identifiable patterns should be used in every overwriting layer to make it hard for attackers to decipher and discover the original information. Ideally, the last and final layer should comprise of zeros for added security. Meanwhile, some "Secure Erase" programs have option for erasing and overwriting select files.

Similarly, although a CD or DVD could be effectively destroyed by wrapping it in a paper towel and rending it, there are hardware devices that erase them by marring their surface. While others practically shred the storage media, some puncture a pattern of holes on the writable surface. Still, some paper shredders can shred CDs and DVDs, also.

6.3 BLUETOOTH CONNECTIVITY AND RELEVANT SECURITY MEASURES - This kind of connectivity is for linking two or more devices that embed Bluetooth technology. For the devices to be linked together, they do not necessarily have to be online; all that is required is that they are switched on and their Bluetooth feature enabled for wireless communication.

As a wireless communication standard, Bluetooth technology relies on short-range radio frequency and when enabled, devices incorporating the technology can communicate within a specific distance or radius. For instance, that is why without cable links, a computer could be operated with a wireless keyboard; a wireless earpiece is used to talk on a mobile phone; data virtually transferrable from one device to another; etc.

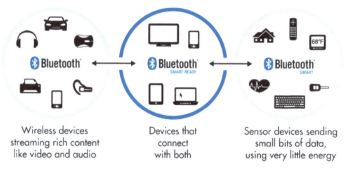

| Wireless devices streaming rich content like video and audio | Devices that connect with both | Sensor devices sending small bits of data, using very little energy |

While two or more Bluetooth technology embedded electronic devices within certain rradius can communicate wirelessly, there are security concerns. **Diagram credit:** bluetooth.com

Many manufacturers make devices like mobile phones, computers and personal digital assistants (PDAs) that enable Bluetooth connectivity. And as usual, there are security concerns ranging from minor to serious. For instance, all it takes for a target's data to be compromised, corrupted, stolen or lost is for a criminal to simply "detect" his or her Bluetooth device.

And in cyber parlance, "bluesnarfing" is the crime of an attacker using a Bluetooth connection to steal data off a target's Bluetooth enabled device. One other way a target could be vulnerable to attack is by falling for inducement from suspects to send information over Bluetooth connection to someone.

However, usage of Bluetooth technology could be secured with appropriate configuration and precautions. For instance, a user can take advantage of its use of key authentication as well as data encryption even though many Bluetooth devices rely on short numeric PIN numbers instead of more secure passwords or passphrases. To substantially mitigate your vulnerability:

6.3.1 **Disable Bluetooth** when you are not using it to transfer information between devices. Disabling it will prevent illegal or unauthorized access.

6.3.2 **When enabled, use Bluetooth in "hidden" mode** to make it "undiscoverable". Though active, the hidden mode prevents other Bluetooth devices from picking your radio signal by chance or casual attempt. This does not, however, hinder devices that have already been legitimately "paired" from discovering each other and communicating. Even in hidden mode, devices that have earlier been "paired" will always recognize each other with no need for rediscovery before communicating.

6.3.3 **Be careful where you use Bluetooth** because when pairing devices or in discoverable mode, especially in public wireless "hotspots", the risk of a criminal intercepting your connection is greater than when you are elsewhere like home or car.

6.3.4 **Evaluate and take advantage of security options** or features that you can tailor to meet your security needs. The first step is finding out the options, including authentication and encryption that your Bluetooth device offers. Subsequently, part of your measures could include ensuring every of your Bluetooth enabled device is configured to require and function only with a secure connection.

Otherwise, leaving certain default settings or enabling certain features heightens the odds of you being attacked.

Chapter 7

PREVENTING AND REACTING TO IDENTITY THEFT

As a crime, identity theft or fraud can leave a trail of adverse financial and emotional consequences. Identity theft is a crime of opportunity that thrives on the basis of information scooped on victims. That is why organizations whose databases on customers are easily accessible for information to mount attacks or sell to marketing companies, are prime targets of criminals.

The internet is making that easier because by hacking into a database, criminals gain access to information on many people rather than on one person at a time. And with enough information from a compromised database, a criminal could impersonate to purchase items, open new accounts or apply for loans, all to a victim's detriment.

Also, one might become a victim of identity theft even without using a computer or criminals hacking into a database. In fact, security of sensitive information like credit card numbers, phone numbers, account numbers, and addresses could be compromised when a wallet is stolen/lost, a phone conversation is eavesdropped, dumpster diving occurred or a restaurant receipt bearing your particulars is picked up. So, here are ways to minimize your risk:

7.1 **TRANSACT BUSINESS WITH CREDIBLE ORGANIZATIONS AND MONITOR ACTIVITIES ON YOUR ACCOUNT** - Before supplying sensitive information, ascertain the actual existence and credibility of an organization with which you are interacting. Criminals do trick unsuspecting targets to divulge sensitive information on malicious web sites devoted to gathering intelligence for crime.

7.2 **RUN UP-TO-DATE SECURITY SOFTWARE AND IMPLEMENT RELEVANT SECURITY MEASURES** - With up-to-date security software and firewalls, protect yourself against viruses and Trojan horses that could steal your data as well as render you vulnerable to further criminal attacks. Also, strong passwords and other security measures should be implemented for a safer multi-layered security arrangement.

7.3 ASCERTAIN PRIVACY POLICIES AND CURTAIL WHAT YOU POST ONLINE - Before supplying sensitive information online, ascertain from the published privacy policies of an organization how your information would be used. Many organizations respect customers' request that their information should not be shared with other companies. Similarly, avoid posting personal data in public fora because criminals are able to piece information together from a variety of sources to facilitate crime.

7.4 RECOVERING FROM IDENTITY THEFT

Although every service provider has its own way of notifying customers when it is discovered that an individual's account has been compromised, be alert to any unusual changes in your account. Meanwhile, unusual charges in your bills, bills for products or services you never ordered, failure to receive bills as usual, strange amounts appearing on your credit report and unexpected rejection of your credit card are all tell-tales signs of criminal tampering with your account.

The policies of financial institutions naturally seek to minimize their liability for losses suffered by their patrons and that makes it potentially costly and stressful for a victim to recover from an identity theft. Therefore, to minimize extent of losses in any infraction, take the following steps as soon as possible:

7.4.1 Contact the financial institutions where you maintain accounts – If a perusal of your periodic credit report or statement of account did not assuage any suspicion, phone your service provider(s) to ascertain if there have been unauthorized transactions on your account(s). Supplement your phone call by sending a letter for a written record of the complaint.

If your fear is confirmed, close affected accounts to prevent further unauthorized transactions and where credit cards are involved, have a fraud alert placed on your credit reports to forestall opening of new accounts without verification.

7.4.2 Intimate law enforcement agencies – For a formal or official record of the incident, file a report with the local police and other related law enforcement agencies.

7.4.3 Consider and act on any other information that could be at risk – It may be necessary for you to contact other agencies depending on what information was stolen. For instance, theft of a wallet containing a whole lot of vital documents would require each and every issuing authority being alerted on the loss of any document they issued.

Chapter 8

TELEPHONE SECURITY

Smartphones and tablets are increasingly being used to perform the same functions as personal computers. Therefore, as mini-computers and mini-broadcasting stations, cell phones are not impervious to the same threats facing wireless computing. In fact, the risk of illegally accessing your device escalates when on the internet or a network accessible by criminals.

Neither is the quest for greater functionality in preference for more security, helping matters. In fact, the continual integration of numerous features into smart phones for increased functionality is regrettably trading off security.

Smart phones and other wireless electronic devices hold vast amounts of sensitive information; hence attractive and strategic targets for criminals. So, caution is advised!
Pic credit: articles.bplans.com and handsonbanking.org, Nitin Bhatnagar

Amongst other risks, that renders most cell phones vulnerable to being remotely turned "on" without users' knowledge. Specifically, from safe distances with specialist equipment, criminals could covertly have cell phones bugged, penetrated for reading/downloading of files, turned to viewing units, new channels opened on them, get infected with malware or used as conduit to infect their network(s).

Another risk is that when cell phones transmit, they could have their ID numbers cloned for use in crime just like their vulnerability to geo-locating endangers users' security.

Similarly, because public phone systems are designed for efficiency and not security, they are vulnerable. In addition to newer methods facilitated by off-site equipment readily sourced off-shelf, all the older methods of bugging landlines are still operational. Worse, users' penchant for convenience at the expense of security, is giving even amateur criminals leeway to easily monitor unencrypted analogue cordless or cell phone calls.

On the whole, it is obvious that mobile devices have become attractive as strategic targets for criminals because they can hold vast amounts of sensitive information. That expectedly puts individuals and society at large at risk of dire consequences. It is therefore, important for users to exercise utmost caution when using smart phones and other wireless electronic devices.

When shopping, banking, or supplying sensitive information online, take all the precautions that you do with your personal computer. Basically, your choice of cell phone model should make for home-screen locking either by a password or biometric. As well, attention should be paid to physical security because their portability risks outright theft.

8.1   MODES OF TELEPHONE ATTACKS

With your smart phone or tablet being more or less a full-fledged computer, it is vulnerable to:

1. **Service Abuse** – Attackers could infect your phone with a malware for illegal access to services at your expense.

2. **Enticement to a Malicious Website** – Apart from standard phishing attacks, criminals do send text messages to cell phones, purportedly from credible companies. The text messages could be persuading you to visit a malicious website to resolve a problem with your account or access a service to which you have been subscribed without your consent. Should you fall for such

gimmick, you could be lured into supplying sensitive information or downloading a malware.

3. **Deployment of your Cell Phone in an attack** – Sometimes, attackers take control of a victim's telephone service as a canon folder to attack others. This conceals the criminals' identity while enabling them to broaden the scope of an attack.

4. **Access to an Online Account details** – With smart phones being used like computers for online transactions, an attacker who hacks into a phone could gather your account information for criminal usage either personally or for sale.

5. **Social Engineering and Phishing** – On the one hand, social engineering attack entails an attacker using human interaction (social skills) to secure or compromise sensitive information about an organization.

To succeed, attackers sound unassuming and respectable while actually pretending to be a new employee, maintenance worker or researcher. By eliciting responses to various questions or from different sources within an organization, an attacker could piece together enough information for compromising an organization's network.

On the other hand, phishing is a form of social engineering that uses emails or malicious websites to solicit sensitive information while posing as a credible organization. An attacker, for instance, could purport to be sending an email from a legitimate financial organization requesting information for account reconciliation or update. The gullible suffers the consequences of their accounts being infiltrated with the very information they supplied.

Apart from impersonating financial institutions, criminals purport to be charitable organizations while taking undue advantage of special times of the year or events like natural disasters, epidemics/health scares, holidays, etc. to solicit for donations or sensitive information with which to perpetuate crime. Therefore, do not supply sensitive information to anyone or organization whose identity and credibility are in doubt.

8.2 SECURITY OF DATA AND COMMUNICATION OVER THE PHONE - New functional features are rapidly emerging than advancements in security. Therefore, pay attention to cell phone news to ascertain security of credit card swipe, mobile banking/ticketing, keyless entry, removable memory, internal hard drives, sender-to-receiver video, TV, etc. before purchasing a particular model.

Also, optimize your security settings accordingly when using rented cell phones abroad because some foreign digital cell phone technologies are not only different but use less encryption and therefore, vulnerable to eavesdropping among other risks. Also:

1. **Prevent Unauthorized Physical Access** - Cell phones are prone to loss/theft because of their portability and a physical access could make it easier for an attacker to extract information. Therefore, steps should be taken to mitigate that risk. Neither give room for unauthorized access to your device nor store sensitive contact numbers and data inside.

2. **Beware of what you say on the Phone** – Especially where sensitive information is involved, think before you talk. If you fear your children or house-helps might disclose vital information in your absence, give them a form to take down callers' particulars for you to call back later.

Where necessary turn off your phone, preferably with battery removed after notifying callers that you are receiving only voice messages. This would leave you the discretion of making live calls.

3. **Decide on use of VOIP at home** – Voice Over Internet Protocol (VOIP) is presently known to reveal a user's telephone number and Internet address. Therefore, decide on not using it until the security standard improves.

4. **Report Suspicions to the Police or Service Provider** – A repeated pattern of wrong numbers/anonymous calls might be efforts to determine who is where and when. Also, depending on the details, some threat calls might be assault crimes. These should be reported to the police and your service provider for security and technical reviews respectively. Any regular pattern of noises when calls go through should be similarly handled.

5. **Avoid publishing your Contact Information** – For control over the category of people that could have access to you, avoid indiscriminate publishing of your email address and cell phone number. Otherwise, attackers who often use special software to browse websites for contact information would automatically collect yours.

6. **Be Wary of Requests for Information** – Be suspicious of unsolicited phone calls or email messages asking for sensitive information. If any information must be supplied or provided to enquirers, their identity and security of their website should first of all be established.

7. **Be Suspicious of links in Email or Text Messages** – Links in emails and text messages may appear legitimate but could actually guide you to malicious websites. Therefore, suspect URLs sent via unsolicited emails or text messages.

8. **Exercise Caution about Downloadable Software** – Avoid free downloading of files from sites that you do not trust because they could be baits to infect your device with malicious codes.

Ascertain any claim of a safe website from presence or otherwise of a genuine website certificate. In the end, when you decide to download a file, consider saving it first and scanning for viruses before opening.

9. **Keep Software up to date** – Whenever a vendor releases updates for your system software, install them promptly to forestall attackers exploiting known vulnerabilities.

10. **Optimize Security Settings and Use Strong Passwords** – Take advantage of the security features offered on your device. Also, select strong passwords that will be difficult for criminals to crack with a separate password for each program or device. Meanwhile, never enable any option which could allow your device to remember a password.

11. **Prevent Cloning of your ID Number** – Although digital phones are more difficult to clone than analogue models, a research indicates that cell phone cloning by criminals is much more prevalent on interstate highways, airport access roads or in airport parking lots.

Therefore, avoid using cell phones at those places. And to detect any cloning early enough, review your bills and promptly clarify any suspicious charges with your service provider.

12. **Encrypt your Data** – Data encryption forestalls unauthorized access to data even after a device is physically violated. So, if your device has data encryption capability, seize the advantage to secure your data. Of course you must not forget the passwords protecting the encryption; otherwise your data could become inaccessible and lost.

13. **Disable Remote Connectivity when Travelling** – When traveling or shopping online be mindful of

the wireless networks you use. Avoid using open Wi-Fi networks at places like airports, coffee shops and other public locations because they aid attackers to intercept sensitive information supplied in online transactions.

However, if you must use your device while travelling to check, say, your bank balance or make an online purchase, turn off your device's Wi-Fi connection and rely on your mobile device's cellular internet connectivity.

Similarly, disable Bluetooth connectivity when not used for hands-free talking or external keyboards because cyber attackers could pair with a phone's open Bluetooth connection to steal sensitive information.

14. **Mind Where you Charge your Cell Phone** - Do not plug your mobile device to a charging station or computer at public places like an airport terminal or a shared computer at a library over which you have no control. Otherwise, your sensitive data could be stolen or a malware installed on your device.

8.3 **WHAT TO DO IF AN ONLINE ACCOUNT IS COMPROMISED** - If you notice that your online account has been hacked, call the bank, store or credit card company that hosts the account. Reporting fraud in a timely manner minimizes the negative impact and lessens your personal liability. You should also change any account password associated with a compromised mobile device, using another computer that you control.

The virtual connectivity hallmark of cellular or wireless technology has deepened the computer concept with greater reliance on portable computing devices like cell phones and tablets. But there are mounting corresponding risks to individuals and organizations who besides own losses, are now liable for collateral harm emanating from attacks on their devices or networks.

That calls for adequate safeguards and good cyber security habits to secure your computing devices from accidental or intentional misuse.

Specifically, the security features of your devices should be upgraded periodically to substantially mitigate all known vulnerabilities. As well, mode(s) of internet connectivity, email services, browsing habits and various electronic identities should be reviewed periodically.

Above all, be cautious about the sort of information on yourself or organization that you post online because there is no such thing as anonymity on the Internet. Otherwise, supplying certain information online could facilitate criminal attacks. While there could be no 100% protection, adopting tested measures can considerably minimize your vulnerability online.

Bibliography

1. Facebook + WhatsApp = The Ultimate Spying Machine? Bernard Marr, 2014, LinkedIn, USA
2. Facebook Data Mining Tool Uncovers Your Life, Mirko Zorz, 2013, Help Net Security, Hrvatska
3. Why Facebook Scandal is the Worst of All, Paul Wagenseil, Tom's Guide, 2018, USA
4. Mark Zuckerberg Apologies for Facebook's Data Scandal in Full-page Newspaper Ads, Nick Statt, 2018, theverge.vom, USA
5. Cook speaks at Beijing Forum following Facebook Controversy, Bloomberg News, David Ramli, 2018, USA
6. How Changing Technology Affects Security, Bruce Schneier, 2015, Wired, USA
7. Cybersecurity becomes a Top Priority after Data Breaches, Richard Blackwell, 2014, The Globe and Mail Inc, USA
8. Internet of Things – Potential Security Risks, Natalie Novitski, 2014, IHLS, Israel
9. How Anonymous are You?, Mindi McDowell, Allen Householder, Matt Lytle, 2010, US-CERT, USA

10. The Definitive Guide to Facebook Security, Robert Siciliano, 2014, ID Theft Security, USA
11. LinkedIn Feature Exposes Email Addresses, Brian Krebs, 2014, Krebson Security, USA
12. Staying Safe on Social Network Sites, Mindi McDowell, 2011, US-CERT, USA
13. Using Instant Messaging and Chat Rooms Safely, Mindi McDowell, Allen Householder, 2009, US-CERT, USA
14. Think Deleted Text Messages Are Gone Forever? Think Again, Tom Kaneshige, 2014, CIO, USA
15. Apple's Reputation for Software Security a 'Myth': Expert, Andre Mayer, 2014, CBC News, USA
16. Public Hotspots Are a Privacy and Security Minefield: Shield Yourself, Kurt Marko, 2014, Forbes, USA
17. Don't's and Do's when using Public Wi-Fi, Robert Siciliano, 2015, ID Theft Security, USA
18. Be Cautious When Using Wi Fi, Robert Siciliano, 2015, ID Theft Security, USA
19. 5 Information Security Breaches You've Never Heard About...But Should Have, Sue Poremba, 2014, Info Security Orion SAS, UK
20. Leaked NSA Documents Reveal the Best Way to Stay Anonymous Online, James Cook, 2014, Business Insider, UK
21. 10 Tips to Stay Safe Online, Robert Sicilano, 2014, ID Theft Security, USA
22. DHS 'Dos and Don'ts' on Cybersecurity, Meg King, 2014, The Hill, USA
23. Cyber Security for Electronic Devices, Mindi McDowell and Matt Lytle, 2011, US-CERT, USA
24. Good Security Habits, Mindi McDowell and Allen Householder, 2009, US-CERT, USA
25. Safeguarding Your Data, Mindi McDowell, 2006, US-CERT, USA
26. Guidelines for Publishing Information Online, Mindi McDowell, et al, 2005, US-CERT, USA
27. Avoiding the Pitfalls of Online Trading, Mindi McDowell, 2011, US-CERT, USA
28. Shopping Safely Online, Mindi McDowell and Monica Maher, 2010, US-CERT, USA
29. Effectively Erasing Files, Mindi McDowell and Matt Lytle, 2013, US-CERT, USA

30. Exploring the Dangers of a Mobile Lifestyle, Zeljka Zorz, 2013, Kaspersky Lab, USA

31. Cyber Threats to Mobile Devices, 2010, US-CERT, USA

32. Mobile Security Concerns Largely Ignored, Despite Threat, Nathan Eddy, 2014, QuinStreet Inc, USA

33. Contactless Payments - Researcher Intercepts Card Data from a Metre Away, Lee Munson, 2013, Naked Security, USA

34. What are Skimming Devices and Cloned Cards? Robert Siciliano, 2015, LinkedIn, USA

35. Want to Spy on Someone? It's Easier Than Ever, Colleen Kane, 2013, CNBC, USA

36. Mobile Security: Threats and Preventive Measures, Nitin Bhatnagar, 2015, LinkedIn, USA

37. Mobile Security: Four Ways to Protect Your Network, 2013, Malcovery Security. LLC, USA

38. Holiday Traveling with Personal Internet-enabled Devices, Amanda Parente , 2011, US-CERT, USA

39. Protecting Portable Devices: Data Security, Mindi McDowell and Matt Lytle, 2011, US-CERT, USA

40. Protecting Portable Devices: Physical Security, Mindi McDowell, 2011, US-CERT, USA

41. Security of Wireless Networks, Mindi McDowell, et al, 2011, US-CERT, USA

42. What is your company's information security exposure? Are you "covered" or are you "naked?" Matthew Goche and John Beattie, 2014, Forbes, USA

43. Most Security Executives lack Confidence in their Security Posture, 2015, Help Net Security, Hrvatska

44. Data Breaches: How to Protect Your Business from Internal Threats, Robert Siciliano, 2014, ID Theft Security, USA

45. Underpaid Employees Are a Cybersecurity Risk, Allison Schrager, 2014, Businessweek, USA

46. The Insider versus the Outsider: Who Poses the Biggest Security Risk, Chris Stoneff, 2015, Help Net Security, Hrvatska

47. Six Technical Measures to Mitigate the Insider Threat, Brian Contos, 2015, CXO Media Inc., USA

48. Agency IT Security Handbook: Operation Controls,_IT Security Systems Version 2.0, 2001

49. Understanding Your Computer: Operating Systems, Mindi McDowell and Chad Dougherty, 2010, US-CERT, USA

50. Evaluating your Web Browser's Security Settings, Mindi McDowell and Jason Rafall, 2013, US-CERT, USA

51. Securing Your Web Browser, Will Dormann and Jason Rafail, 2011, US-CERT, USA

52. Reviewing End-User License Agreements, Mindi McDowell, 2011, US-CERT, USA

53. Understanding Patches,_Mindi McDowell, 2009, US-CERT, USA

54. Browsing Safely: Understanding Active Content and Cookies, Mindi McDowell and Jason Rafail, 2011, US-CERT, USA

55. Understanding Internationalized Domain Names, Mindi McDowell et al, 2008, US-CERT, USA

56. Understanding Website Certificates, Mindi McDowell and Matt Lytle, 2010, US-CERT, USA

57. Understanding ISPs, Mindi McDowell, 2011, US-CERT, USA

58. Small Office/Home Office Router Security, 2013, US-CERT, USA

59. Recognizing and Avoiding Spyware,_Mindi McDowell and Matt Lytle, 2011, US-CERT, USA

60. Ransomware and the Importance of Everyday Cyber Security Vigilance, Spencer Coursen, 2015, Coursen Security Group, USA

61. Ransomware Looming As Major Long-Term Threat, Dennis Fisher, 2015, Threatpost News, USA

62. Botnets Turn Victims of Cyber Crime into Unknowing Accomplices, Aris Demos, 2013, Global Digital Forensics, USA

63. Understanding Hidden Threats: Rootkits and Botnets, Mindi McDowell, 2011, US-CERT, USA

64. Understanding Hidden Threats: Corrupted Software Files, Mindi McDowell, 2011, US-CERT, USA

65. Avoiding Social Engineering and Phishing Attacks, Mindi McDowell, 2009, US-CERT, USA

66. Dealing with Cyberbullies, Mindi McDowell, 2011, US-CERT, USA

67. Identifying Hoaxes and Urban Legends, Mindi McDowell and Allen Householder, 2013, US-CERT, USA
68. Understanding Anti-Virus Software, Mindi McDowell and Allen Householder, 2009, US-CERT, USA
69. Understanding Firewalls, Mindi McDowell and Allen Householder, 2015, US-CERT, USA
70. Coordinating Virus and Spyware Defense, Mindi McDowell and Matt Lytle, 2009, US-CERT, USA
71. Recovering from Viruses, Worms, and Trojan Horses, Mindi McDowell, 2011, US-CERT, USA
72. Email and Communication, Mindi McDowell and Allen Householder, 2011, US-CERT, USA
73. FBI Sounds Alarm Again on Business Email Compromise Threat, Jai Vijayan, 2015, LinkedIn, USA
74. Understanding Your Computer: Email Clients, Mindi McDowell, 2010, US-CERT, USA
75. Benefits and Risks of Free Email Services, Mindi McDowell and Allen Householder, 2011, US-CERT, USA
76. Email Scams, Tricks, Hacks, Cheats, and Tweaks That Everyone Should Know, Steve Mierzejewski, 2015, Twitter, USA
77. The Little Book of Big Scams, 2013, Metropolitan Police Service, UK
78. Don't Use Administrator Accounts Unnecessarily! 2015, Swan Island Networks, Inc., USA
79. Using Caution with Email Attachments, Mindi McDowell and Allen Householder, 2011, US-CERT, USA
80. Password and Algorithm Security, T. O'Connor, 2012, MegaLinks in Criminal Justice, USA
81. Choosing and Protecting Passwords, Mindi McDowell, et al, 2011, US-CERT, USA
82. Understanding Digital Signatures, Mindi McDowell and Allen Householder, 2009, US-CERT, USA
83. Here's Everywhere You Should Enable Two-Factor Authentication Right Now, Whitson Gordon, 2014, LinkedIn, USA
84. Supplementing Passwords, Mindi McDowell et al, 2011, US-CERT, USA
85. Understanding Encryption, Mindi McDowell et al, 2010, US-CERT, USA
86. Reducing Spam, Mindi McDowell and Allen Householder, 2011, US-CERT, USA

87. The Modus Operandi of Hacking, T. O'Connor, 2012, MegaLinks in Criminal Justice, USA
88. Which are the most notorious hacking groups? Newsdesk, 2015, IHLS, Israel
89. How to Protect Yourself from Evil Hackers, Sarah Jacobsson Purewal, 2014, Men'sHealth, USA
90. Protecting Your Accounts from Hackers, Temitayo Famutimi, 2013, The Punch, Nigeria
91. Regaining Control of Hacked Accounts, Temitayo Famutimi, 2013, The Punch, Nigeria
92. Post-Data Breach Reputation Building, Robert Siciiliano, 2014, LinkedIn, USA
93. Preventing and Responding to Identity Theft, Mindi McDowell, 2008, US-CERT, USA
94. Understanding Denial-of-Service Attacks, Mindi McDowell, 2009, US-CERT, USA
95. Understanding Voice over Internet Protocol (VoIP), Mindi McDowell, 2008, US-CERT, USA
96. Risks of File-Sharing Technology, Mindi McDowell, et al, 2011, US-CERT, USA
97. Understanding Bluetooth Technology, Mindi McDowell and Matt Lytle, 2010, US-CERT, USA
98. USB Drives have serious Security Flaws, Robert Siciliano, 2014, Huffington Post, USA
99. Using Caution with USB Drives, Mindi McDowell, 2011, US-CERT, USA
100. How to see and boot off Someone Using Your WiFi, Robert Siciliano, 2014, LinkedIn, USA
101. Cover Your Webcam, Charles Jennings, 2013, Swan Island Networks, USA
102. Insider Threats – Is Your Organization Safe? Oliver Brdiczka, 2014, Computerworld, USA
103. 73,000 Security Cameras Viewable Online Due to Use of Default Passwords, David Bisson, 2014, Tripwire, USA
104. Defending Cell Phones and PDAs against Attacks, Mindi McDowell, 2011, US-CERT, USA
105. Which smartphone is the most secure? Spencer McIntyre, 2012, CSO Online, USA
106. What Secrets Your Phone is Sharing About You, Elizabeth Dwoskin, 2014, Wall Street Journal, USA

107. A Quarter of Smartphone Users Fail to Protect Privacy, Survey Shows, Alexandra Gheorghe, 2014, HotforSecurity, USA

108. The 6 Steps for Keeping Your Phone Secure, Matthew, 2014, The Safe Shop, UK

109. How to Make Secure Calls Online? Lyudmila Kozachok, 2015, LinkedIn, USA

110. Is Your Smartphone being Tracked? Agent Cooper, 2014, Geek Squad, UK

111. Mysterious Fake Cellphone Towers Are Intercepting Calls All Over the US, Jack Dutton, 2014, Business Insider, USA

112. Spy Cell Towers: A New Service is Hunting for You, Barry Levine, 2015, Venture Beat, USA

113. Even Cellular Providers Spy on their Clients, Dov Lachman, 2014, IHLS, Israel

114. Mobile Carriers Spying on Users, Robert Siciliano, 2014, ID Theft Security, USA

115. Swindlers Use Telephones, With Internet's Tactics, Nick Wingfieldjan, 2014, New York Tines, USA

116. 5 Alarming Things that can be Undeleted from Your Phone Using Police Software, Matt Carter, 2014, Venture Beat, USA

117. Using Your Mobile to Protect You from Criminals, Robert Siciliano, 2014, ID Theft Security, USA

118. How to Protect Yourself from Caller ID Spoofing, Andrew Swoboda, 2015, Tripwire, USA

119. Keeping Children Safe Online, Mindi McDowell and Allen Householder, 2011, US-CERT, USA

www.ingramcontent.com/pod-product-compliance
Lightning Source LLC
Chambersburg PA
CBHW041143050326
40689CB00001B/466